THE HIDDEN HURT Man

MELVIN C. DAWSON, JR.

THE HIDDEN HURT MAN

Copyright ©2016 by Melvin C. Dawson, Jr.

All rights reserved. No part of this book may be reproduced, copied, stored or transmitted in any form or by any means – graphic, electronic, or mechanical, including photocopying, recording, or information storage and retrieval systems without the prior written permission of Melvin C. Dawson, Jr. or Hope of Vision Publishing except where permitted by law.

All biblical references are from the King James Version (KJV) translation bible unless otherwise noted. Additional references are from the Amplified Translation (AMP) or Message Translation (MSG). All rights reserved.

HOV Publishing a division of HOV, LLC.
www.hovpub.com
hopeofvision@gmail.com

Cover Design: HOV Design Solutions
Editor/Proofreader: Bettye Walker

Write the Author Melvin C. Dawson, Jr. at:
Email: melvindawsonministries@yahoo.com

For more information about special discounts for bulk purchases, please contact Bridget Moore at Cathedral of Praise ICFM, Post Office Box 570303, Miami, FL 33257. Call 786-599-1796 or email: cathedralofpraiseicfm@yahoo.com.

ISBN 978-1-942871-16-3
Library of Congress Control Number: 2016958349

10 9 8 7 6 5 4 3 2 1

Printed in the United States of America

DEDICATION

I dedicate this book to my mother, Evangelist Annie Dawson, who has proven to be the greatest prayer warrior I have ever known (as well as a "walking Bible", for there's not a scripture she cannot find when I'm having a "senior moment"). Even in her own health challenges, she has been, and always will be, my Number 1 Fan...And she admits that!!!! Mom I pray that I have always made you proud in all of my endeavors for Christ. You taught me what it means to be committed to the clarion call of God, and to not stop until your work and assignment is complete.

Thanks Mom, I Love You!

Acknowledgements

It goes without saying, there is no way I could have written this book without the help of my Lord and Savior, Jesus Christ. He is my strength and my guiding light, and the inspiration by which I exist. As the Apostle Paul writes, "For in Him we live and move and have our being; as even some of your [own] poets have said, for we are also His offspring." (Act 17:28, AMP). I am intrigued more and more about Christ as I devote my life and journey in full commitment to Him.

Although you can never have anyone greater than Christ as your inspirational strength, my lovely wife, Kay, is a close second. She has proven to be such a motivating and empowering force of support and energy for me in completing this book, and I salute her for everything she is and has done. Of course, this includes our children who are all grown up—Aryelle, 28, Melvin III, 26 and Ahkeem, 24—who continuously remind me that I am the greatest inspiration in their eyes. How can I *not* succeed with that kind of support? Speaking of family, I must confess that life became more real in September 2014 when I experienced congenital heart failure. It is only through the grace and help of God, and the support of my family that I found a new reason to live, to make an impact on the world while I am still alive.

My church family (Cathedral of Praise Daytona Beach since November 2014 and Cathedral of Praise Miami where it all began on September 28, 1997) I thank you for your support on so many different levels, especially financially. You all have sown valuable seeds into my life and ministry. Like my loving family (Kay, Rel, Mel, and Keemie, the terms of endearment names I use to describe my family), you believed in every dream God has given me. You have allowed me to be Overseer, Pastor, Recording Artist, Author, Playwright, Actor, a member of the Board of Visitors at Bethune-Cookman University (Daytona Beach, Florida), Counselor, Minister of Music, Instructor of Christian Education and Founder of several ministerial training symposiums. You never ceased to remain faithfully committed to your own calling and work while faithfully supporting me. I love you all.

To Nichole ("Nikki") for typing the manuscript and for all the late night chats when I needed to bounce a thought off you that I was struggling with, thank you! To Alvarae, my cousin and administrative assistant (Cathedral of Praise Daytona Beach), thanks a million for all the times I made you sit and listen to me read a paragraph or two, and then criticize your critique! To my two closest pastoral friends, Bishop Tiangello Hill (Cathedral of Praise Ministries, Albany, GA) and Pastor Michael White (Litman Cathedral HOGSIC, Albany, GA), who I bugged continuously about ideas for this book and who coincidently happen to both pastor in Albany, GA (the birthplace of the legendary Ray Charles). And there are at least twenty other pastors that I must thank (you know who you are), who I bounced more than a few ideas and thoughts off of their intellectual insight. To Dr. Charles Booth, Senior Pastor-Teacher of Mount Olivet Baptist Church in Columbus, Ohio, who during the 2014 Men's Gathering and Training Session at a Kingdom Connection Fellowship Fresh Power Convocation (Bishop

Jerome H. Ross, Sr., Presiding Prelate), not only spoke into my spirit but allowed me to share the infancy seed of this book to his class and ultimately inspired me to write it. It was my full intent to have him write the Forward to this book but I dropped the ball, as time slipped away from me in an attempt to meet my publisher's deadline. I hope you can write the next one, for I will write again!

Special thanks to Bishop Victor T. Curry, Founder and Senior Pastor-Teacher of New Birth Baptist Church and the Cathedral of Faith Miami, Florida, who has maintained his promise to always be my friend. It was a pact he and I made almost twenty years ago, during our humble beginnings, and he has remained true to his word. Thanks for believing in me on so many levels. Even in your God-given greatness, you remain faithful and humble to your call and anointing. It is my greatest pleasure and reward to call you friend.

For anyone I may have missed—and you know that you helped me complete this book—thank you from the bottom of my heart. In the words of the Apostle Paul to the church at Philippi, I pray that "God [will] supply all your needs according to his riches in glory by Christ Jesus." (Philippians 4:19).

CONTENT

FOREWORD 13
INTRODUCTION 15

Chapter 1: WHERE DO OUR TEARS GO? 19
    Basal Tears 19
    Reflex Tears 19
    Emotional Tears 19
    The Root of Our Emotions 20
    Alternatives for Coping 22

Chapter 2: SEX: THE PAINFUL OUTLET 25
    Sexual Transference 27
    Fruitful Sexual Relationships 28
    Sexual Stress and Duress 29
    The Bonds of Sexual Communication 30

Chapter 3: GREEN-EYED MONSTER CALLED JEALOUSY 33
    Root Cause of Jealousy 35
    Sovereign Jealousy vs. Human Jealousy 36
    Three Forms of Jealousy 37

Chapter 4: BOYS NIGHT OUT 41
    A Comparative Study: "Girl's Night Out" 41
    A Comparative Study: "Boys Night Out" 43
    A Man's Competitive Nature 44

Chapter 5: THE GOD FACTOR   49
    Argument #1: "The Missing Father Syndrome"   50
    Argument #2: "The Preacher Perception"   53
    Argument #3: "The Sensitive Worshipper"   56

Chapter 6: THE CURSE OF IMPOTENCY   59
    Blindness   62
    Halt   65
    Withered   68

Chapter 7: I'M SICK OF DENZEL   71
    "D" (Dapper Effect)   72
    "E" (Electrifying Spirit)   72
    "N" (Nemesis Nature of Narcissistic Neglect)   75
    "Z" (Zeus Effect)   75
    "E" (Eeriness of Expectations)   77
    "L" (Luxurious Leisure)   78

Chapter 8: DAMN THE MAN CAVE   81
    Problem #1: The Cave Man   82
    Problem #2: Family Separation   84
    Problem #3: The Sinfulness of the Cave   86
    Problem #4: The Battle of Domestic Power   87
    Problem #5: The Place of Insecurity   89
    Problem #6: The Haven of Isolation   90
    Problem #7: The Man Cave Imprisonment   91

Chapter 9: THE RELATIONSHIP DILEMMA: THE CRACKED RIB   95
    R (Relationship Responsibility)   102
    I (Insatiable Interest)   103
    B (Barricade Busting)   103

**Chapter 10: NO MORE HURT: LETTING
    GOD FIND YOU**   107
    Principle #1: God Is Calling You   111
    Principle #2: Responding to His Call   113
    Principle #3: Open and Honest Dialogue   116
    Surrendering All To God   119

Chapter 11: THE BONUS TRACK   133
    I'm Laughing But It Ain't Funny   133
    A Bomb Is Ticking Inside   134
    There's No Doctor for This: The Fear of
    Seeking Help   138
    The Religion of Self-Preservation   140

REFERENCES   145

FOREWORD

Most people who are avid readers typically stand outside the manuscript, assessing and evaluating the work with an almost indifferent posture. Occasionally we encounter a work that draws us into the text and we become immersed. But the book, *The Hidden Hurt Man*, is very different. This book gets into you and that is the key ingredient to actually reaching those who know far too well how to hide.

As a pastor, I grapple with the numerous challenges and complexities we face: Senseless deaths, violence, racism and economic disparity. The list just seems endless. It is always encouraging to meet a work that does a work in me. Melvin Dawson has compiled a thought-provoking text to pose the questions that stimulate the conversation that every man should have with himself. The genius of this work is—while many attempt to provide help—the real help is to inspire genuine dialogue, first with oneself and then hopefully onto real conversations with the Father who has the remedy for all our hurts.

Not every writer has the ability to broach a subject with such audacious abandon—to delve into the dark areas where the faint of heart merely brush over and leave untouched. Melvin fearlessly broaches the real issues of today and holds nothing back. He firmly presents his case leaving the reader inspired and intrigued. It reminds me of open heart surgery where the chest is literally sawed open by a skilled surgeon. Once inside, the surgeon makes the necessary repairs and mends the patient with a favorable, lifesaving result.

This is a book for real men. It will be a catalyst to break up the previously dormant and neglected hearts of countless men, allowing a true and meaningful change that will undoubtedly and positively affect not only the men who are hiding but the women who love them, the children who need them, and the world that awaits them.

Bishop Victor T. Curry
Founding Senior Pastor
New Birth Baptist Church Cathedral of Faith International
Miami, FL

INTRODUCTION

Scripture records a profound statement of truth: *"Man that is born of woman is of a few days and full of trouble."* (Job 14:1, NKJV). Despite this plausibility truth, Job does not clarify how men are to deal with this "fullness" of trouble. As such, most men ignore the "elephant in the room" and have yet to figure out how to survive the overwhelming realities and struggles of being a *Hidden Hurt Man*.

From their earliest childhood memories, throughout puberty and beyond into boyhood, men are taught to never cry. And yet, they are expected to "be a man" and to take on manly responsibilities without having been given any instructions on what to do or how to handle their emotions during stressful and demanding times. Afterwards comes the "pression" family: **Oppression** (the state of being kept down by unjust use of force or authority), **Suppression** (the conscious exclusion of unacceptable thoughts or desires), and **Depression** (a mental state characterized by a pessimistic sense of inadequacy and despondent lack of activity).

This mind-altering, emotionally draining state of mind forces a man into survival mode. Undermining his painful reality is the truth: Men who hide usually hurt. Men who hurt often hide. Men who are both hidden and hurting often masquerade behind a mask of false happiness. It should not come as any surprise then, when men seek the company and brotherhood of other like-minded victims. The great irony of this is they are hiding in the open—hiding within a "maze of visibility," hoping to camouflage themselves from the limitations placed upon them that define what is usual, regular or common.

Why write a book on the *Hidden Hurt Man* when men have become experts at hiding? It certainly is not a tell-all book written for women to discuss the frailties of men (even though in reading it, they will probably gain greater insight into the unspoken perplexities of a man). Neither is it written for the purpose of men to help them come out of a dungeon of obscurity and isolation/ (I addressed that subject in a former book entitled, *The Man In The Hole: Learning to Accept Your Season of Obscured Isolation.*" (Dawson, M., 2013). I wrote this book because far too many men are forced to live beneath their privilege rather than living a life of confidence, freedom and power; because men have been imprisoned by personal hurt and emotional castration forcing them into a false pretense of wellness and wholeness, when they are neither; and because all of these issues have been going on for far too long and are experienced by men during much of their adult life.

How does a man (who, by definition, is deemed an adult male, whose character is meant to be virile and courageously competent, and who is expected to be a husband, lover, boyfriend and confidant to a woman) get to a place where the complex attributes of his manhood are defined and defeated by an inability to express himself emotionally? By an honest examination of the truth? It is my desire that everyone reading this book will become enlightened by the truthful reality that men suffer deeply are in need of help and desperately want to be rescued by someone who cares. And yes, they need your strength and help even though most may never ask for it. Unlike their female counterpart, it is difficult for a man to admit he needs rescuing. Even I have been guilty of traveling in the wrong direction far too long before asking for my wife's help and assistance. It is easy to dismiss these actions as a "man thing" but even I found it hard to admit within the confines of my own private thoughts that I was lost. My inability to admit my mistakes not only delayed my own destination but also the destination of my household and all those who shared in the experience of my journey.

Far too often, men have been guilty of seasonal delays to their households due to their unwillingness to come out of hiding, ask for help and accept being rescued. Some truths and insights shared in this book will bring new revelation to your perspective about men in general. Some will simply confirm why men act the way that they do. Some will make you laugh and some may even make you to cry. Whatever the case may be, I pray that in the end you are made more aware and sensitive of the needs of men who are hiding and hurting. Some of the chapters in this book will bring insight into a man's hiding places, revealing his strengths, inadequacies, and weaknesses in uncomfortable places. From the pressures revealed in "The God Factor" and "I'm Sick of Denzel" to the pain revealed in "Damn the Man Cave" and "Sex: The Painful Outlet," if you approach these pages with an open heart and mind, you may discover some new things about your father, husband, brother, son, lover, your "boo", or even yourself. Where these discoveries take you after that is up to God.

Finally, as a personal disclaimer, this is not an autobiography of my personal life and struggles. Even though admittedly, at the onset of my writing, I experienced my own share of Job's "full troubles" first hand. (Job 14:1). My one and only desire is that no one ends up the same but walks away from this experience better for having taken this journey. Until at last, every man born of a woman can reach a spiritually enlightened place where he honestly and sincerely hurts no more.

CHAPTER: 1
WHERE DO OUR TEARS GO?

There is nothing like a good cry. In fact, crying can actually make you feel better physically and emotionally. In the article, *How Crying Works,* Alia Hoyt examines the basis of our tears from three different perspectives:

Basal Tears

Basal tears are considered *omnipresent* in that they exist to keep our eyes from drying out. The human body produces an average of five to ten ounces of basal tears each day, which drain through the nasal cavity. This is why we often develop a runny nose after crying for any length of time.

Reflex Tears

Reflex tears help protect the human eye from exposure to harsh irritants like smoke, onions, dust and debris. This is achieved through the sensory nerves in your cornea which communicate the presence of an irritant to the brain stem. The brain stem in turn sends hormones to the glands in the eyelids, which causes the eye to produce tears; and thus, ridding the eye of the irritating substance.

Emotional Tears

The third type, which is defined as *emotional tears*, start in the cerebrum where sadness is registered.

The endocrine system is then triggered to release hormones to the ocular area, which in turn causes tears to form. Emotional tears are common to us whenever we are moved by sensations of grief, loss or sadness in one form or another. It is the root of our emotional experiences, however, where every man must begin his journey.

The Root of Our Emotions

One of the initial reasons men hurt so deeply is because they hide rather than confront their feelings when faced with the pressures of life. A man's inability to express his emotional side often results in him internalizing unnecessary hurt, pain and anguish. We become what we are as "hidden hurting" men, trying to cope with the realities of certain experiences that occurred during our childhood. The question we must ask ourselves as men is this: "If we are imprisoned in our minds and programmed not to cry, then where do our tears go?"

Although I was raised in a loving two parent home, surrounded by wholesome Christian values and moral fortitude, I can still remember the frightening words associated with my perception of self and the need to express and release my emotions. (You know, the emotional thoughts and feelings children have after a spanking). If I cried too long, I would hear phrases like: "If you don't hush up all of that crying, I'll give you something to cry about," "Quit crying like a baby," "Man up" or "Don't be a sissy." When you are trying to live up to strong heroic and iconic figures like *Starsky and Hutch*, Steve Austin in *The Six Million Dollar Man*, Richard Rountree as *Shaft,* Samuel L. Jackson (one of my personal favorites), or the coolest Black man to ever live, Billy Dee

Williams, these types of phrases can be deeply debilitating and hurtful. As such, crying is not an option when it comes to male masculinity. This results in men developing a hard core exterior that ultimately works against them.

Where do a man's tears go when he is forced to withhold his emotions? It causes a build up and is forced into other areas of the body. Figuratively speaking, this build up can form "emotional puddles" and "slippery places" that test a man's masculinity and role as a father, husband and man. If a man is incapable of standing in this place to take his rightful place as a father, husband and man, then he can easily lose confidence in himself. This creates a sense of instability where a man begins to "slip in and out" of the relationships he was meant to procreate and give birth to.

Now imagine the evolution of a man who has suffered years of neglect from not knowing how to express his emotions freely? What started out as a small "emotional puddle" can potentially turn into a large "emotional pool," where a man is left drowning as a result of improper "emotional" breathing. "Emotional pools" are like standing water on a flat roof top. If left unaddressed and unattended, it will eventually saturate and penetrate through the protective surface of the roof (a man's emotions). Once this happens, damage occurs to the roof (his emotions) and other essentials like the ceiling, furniture and carpet are destroyed as well. The price to replace and repair the damage done can be costly; and no woman wants to put up with a man who is costly when it comes to his emotions. Some men who are incapable of expressing their emotions find and create outlets to relieve themselves of emotional pain and frustration. Not all outlets are good or healthy. In fact, a man's frustrations can often give rise to expressions that reveal themselves at the most inopportune times.

Alternatives for Coping

There are a number of alternatives for coping with the echoes of the past and dealing with the debilitating thoughts like "men don't cry" and "it is too late to teach an old dog new tricks."

Counseling and Therapy. Counseling is one good option but then a man is faced with the embarrassment of people labeling him as crazy because he goes to a shrink. God forbid if one of his buddies were to find that out. Authors, Richard L. Meth and Robert S. Pasick, in their book, *Men in Therapy: The Challenge of Change*, suggested that "Men [are] considered difficult [when it comes] to [engaging] in psychotherapy, often being described as resistant, unworkable, and unfeeling." (Meth & Pasick, 1990).

My wife, Anita Kay Williams-Dawson, who practices Marriage and Family Therapy, offers the following professional and clinical opinions concerning a man's lack of interest in pursuing counseling and therapy:

> "To defend against unwelcome feelings, many men adopt an attitude of superiority, entitlement and contempt for others. They believe that they are not in pain and it is everyone else who is off. Many men are raised and taught to be the very opposite of

what therapy attempts to pull out of them (emotions), and believe that any signs of sadness or fear is a sign of weakness. Because negative emotions arouse shame and discomfort, many men who attend therapy are there as a result of their wives, girlfriends, significant others, or children threatening them to change or else." (Dawson, K., 2015).

On a positive note, my wife Kay also states that in her time spent as a therapist she has observed that most of the men who attended her therapy sessions eventually admit that the sessions were of great help in helping them to discover themselves and the change needed for their families.

The Church vs. Sports. Many men have lost their zeal when it comes to the "traditional" church. If or when they do seek a "higher power," it is usually under the guise of serving a God who does not require too much change. In the minds of many men, the church makes too many demands on them emotionally. And yet, when it comes to sports and watching football, basketball or baseball, they rarely have any difficulties expressing their emotions.

As a pastor, the church has always been an integral part of my life. Not once have I ever consider it too demanding to cheer loudly for my favorite football team, the Miami Dolphins. During the 2011 NFL season, I was a season ticket holder of eight home games and two pre-season games. I personally experienced the draw on my emotions and what true "emotionalism" really feels like as men of all races and types, ran, screamed, yelled, hugged and shared food and beverages with perfect strangers. Anyone who shared the aqua and orange symbols of the Miami Dolphins was considered a true friend, colleague and fan.

If men can become this emotional over a game, then why not in the church with men who share similar perspectives and challenges? Perhaps the issue is that far too many men view emotionalism in church as something farfetched, belittling and embarrassing; as opposed to the elation of their favorite sport team which puts them at ease, allowing them to freely express their emotions. If a man rejects therapy and refuses to attend church, then where does he go—how can he—openly express himself emotionally? Moreover, if we do not feel comfortable enough to allow our tears to flow outwardly, then where do our tears go?

CHAPTER: 2
SEX: THE PAINFUL OUTLET

"God spoke: 'Let us make human beings in our image, make them reflecting our nature so they can be responsible for the fish in the sea, the birds in the air, the cattle, and yes, Earth itself, and every animal that moves on the face of the Earth'. God created human beings; He created them godlike, reflecting God's nature. He created them male and female. God blessed them: 'Prosper! Reproduce! Fill Earth! Take charge! Be responsible for fish in the sea and birds in the air, for every living thing that moves on the face of Earth'." (Genesis 1:26-28, MBT)

A quick glance at the words spoken by the Holy Trinity in the above passage reminds us that intimacy (sex) was an essential part of God's plan of development for man from the moment of creation. Therefore, it should not come as any surprise when men who are hurting and hiding often use sex as a means of escaping their troubles. Job 14:1 (NKJV) also says, "Man who is born of woman is of a few days and full of trouble." Based on this passage of scripture, we find that men who are hurting and hiding from their troubles are also prone to use sex as a painful outlet. And thus, what is designed to be a pleasurable experience turns out to be short lived because "release" rarely results in "relief."

Some of the questions we must ask ourselves as men are: How can intimacy be a productive form of procreation—multiplying, replenishing, fruitfulness—

when we continue to hide our vulnerabilities? How can we enter into permanent and fulfilling relationships when we continue to hide behind a "James Bond" persona, leaving a trail of seasonal female bodies and holding on to moments that never last beyond a naked expression of sexual stimulation? How can something designed to be good in God's creative plan cause so much pain?

Men who use sex to hide their emotional frustrations are actually no better off than men who are addicted to drugs and alcohol. In a broader sense, using sex to hide emotional frustrations is actually far worse than being addicted to drugs and alcohol because men are entrapped and imprisoned by their own false misrepresentations of passion. In *Every Day for Every Man: 365 Readings for Those Engaged in the Battle,"* authors Stephen Arterburn, Fred Stoeker, and Kenny Luck with Mike Yorkey, introduced three problems associated with an "addictive sex" mindset:

    1) Addictive Sex is Devoid of Intimacy - Sex addicts are utterly self-focused. They cannot achieve genuine intimacy because their self-obsession leaves no room for giving to others.
    2) Addictive Sex is Victimizing - The overwhelming obsession with gratification blinds sex addicts to the harmful effects their behavior is having on others and on themselves.
    3) Addictive Sex Ends in Despair - When "married" couples make love, they are more fulfilled for having had the experience. Addictive sex leaves the participants feeling guilty, regretting the experience. Rather than fulfilling them, it leaves them feeling even emptier.

The authors go on to say that "the escapist nature of addictive sex is often one of the clearest indicators that it is present." (Arterburn, et al., 2005). Again, the man's pain which is attached to the emotional state of his consciousness is the result of "releasing" without finding "relief." After the sexually stimulated moment is over, nothing actually changes. The problem the man had before the sexual encounter is still there after the sexual release. Many extramarital affairs start off with some form of false imagery that the relationship will change their lives for the better. While there may be "special moments" that seem "magical" during the extended time of intimate exhaustion, if the relationship is used as a mechanism for escape from some painful aspect of reality, then the reality will eventually win. By the time the man discovers that he can no longer excuse away the truth of his reality, lives will have been irreparably damaged in some way, shape or form. The one thing Hollywood fails to make evident in all of its wonderfully portrayed, sexually stimulating scenes of the lead star (having his way with as many women as a two hour movie will allow) is the spiritual truth and reality that sex *transfers* spirits. This is why having sex outside of marriage is frowned upon by God.

Sexual Transference

Allow me to explain what is meant by sexually "transferring" spirits. Have you ever hugged someone with a strong scent of perfume or cologne and discovered that after you had departed from their company, the scent of their fragrance lingered in your mind and possibly on your clothes? Well, this is exactly the basis of how the transference of spirits occurs. Whenever you share yourself with someone intimately (sexually), their "spirit" lingers with you and is "emotionally" tied to you, whether good, bad or indifferent. This is what is meant in secular and spiritual circles as "soul ties." Not everyone can handle the spirits that attach themselves through the act of sex. If the man happens to be a person who is hidden and hurting, then the possibility exists that he is also sharing and transferring his vulnerabilities and idiosyncrasies with his partner(s). Truthfully speaking, there is no way of identifying what harm may have been done after they separate from each other.

Who can forget the 1987 box office hit, *Fatal Attraction,* starring Glenn Close, Michael Douglas, and Anne Archer? How a married man's one night stand comes back to haunt him when his estranged lover (who apparently had some major emotional issues) begins to stalk him and his family? Here is a prime example of how shared moments of intimacy (particularly outside of marriage) can ruin relationships. It can also be very difficult to gauge how a person will respond the morning after a sexual encounter. In the movie, Alex (Glenn Close) cannot let go of Dan (Michael Douglas) and will stop at nothing to have him for herself. How far will a person go to get what they want after receiving what they should have never had in the first place? It is difficult to say but questions like this make sex a painful outlet—release but no relief—and, in many instances, equates to added stress.

Fruitful Sexual Relationships

Not all sexual encounters result in painful outlets. A major problem, when it comes to sex, is misunderstanding its place in a relationship. Sex is meant to be the "fruit" of a relationship and not the "root" of it. The *strength* of a wholesome relationship and partnership is that it is built upon a foundation of effective communication. The *art* of successful communication lies in a couple's ability to be open, honest and trustworthy with one another. But when sex is used as an "outlet," there is no open honesty of trust because the relationship is initiated by a selfish ploy to reach a climatic end that is not fulfilling in terms of a long-term relationship. Again, we need to ask ourselves as men how something that was created by God, for the purpose of increase, has resulted in the cause behind so much pain.

Sexual Stress and Duress

Physical pressures associated with emotional stress and duress can also be a contributing factor to painful sexual outlets. Believe it or not, a man's ability to make love is often judged as a part of his personality, which in turn causes a great deal of anxiety as a result of him trying to keep up with his "James Bond" image. Since anxiety which is linked to sexual performance tends to be self-sustaining, the stress level associated with every sexual encounter increases with every failed attempt. Wow, talking about crazy.

Consider the repercussions of the above in light of the following scenario: A man under great stress wants to have sex to relieve his stress. But he finds himself becoming even more stressed as a result of thinking that he will not be able to function at peak performance, with or without the little "blue pill" to assist him. He experiences a "release" but finds no "relief" as a result of the overwhelming pressures associated with this obtrusive level of stress. In contrast, what if the woman he is with has her own idiosyncrasies while engaging in sex? What if these idiosyncrasies result from past traumas associated with rape, molestation and other abusive acts? And what if her former sexual encounters affected not only her mind, body, soul and spirit but also her ability to perform sexually with the same ease depicted on television or in the movies? How does a man trying to cope with his own issues ultimately help a woman who is struggling with her issues as well? Moreover, how does a struggling man handle a woman who has mastered the art of love making (and please forgive me if I am overtly offensive to anyone) with the potential of multiple climatic orgasms and sensual expressions? This in and of itself could cause a hurting man to go into hiding.

The Bonds of Sexual Communication

This brings us to our final topic for this chapter, which is "sexual communication." One of the reasons hurting men resort to hiding, in an attempt to use sex as an outlet, is their inability to communicate with their significant other. (I am forced to reference a "significant other" because most men reject God's mandate of intimacy and sexual intercourse as a "spiritual bond" between a husband and wife, and not merely between a man and woman). As such, the bonds of sexual communication between a man and his wife is reserved under the guise of the two being joined in marriage; as opposed to extramarital affairs that are the result of a "failure to communicate," as suggested by Strother Martin to Paul Newman in the 1967 film, *Cool Hand Luke*.

Many men, especially those who are hurting and hiding, find it extremely difficult to open themselves in honest dialogue with their wives. Especially when it comes to problems they are facing in trying to successfully be a man. (I will talk more about this topic in the chapter, "The Cracked Rib"). Communication becomes even more strained when it occurs during the sexual intimacy. Elaine Fantle Shimberg, author of *Blending Families*, insists that "all relationship problems stem from poor communication skills. [Couples] can't communicate while (always) checking [their] Blackberry, watching TV, or flipping through the sports section." (Shimberg, 1999). And thus, extramarital affairs often serve as an outlet for the lack of attention communicated in the home between a couple.

CHAPTER: 3
GREEN-EYED MONSTER CALLED JEALOUSY

No matter how much a man tries to portray himself as cool, calm, and collected, when he is confronted by the green-eyed monster—otherwise known as jealousy—he usually cannot hide it or hold it in. While it may feel awkward for a man to admit that he experiences this particular "hidden hurt," it is nevertheless important that we talk about this one crucially important issue. According to several popular dictionaries, *jealousy* is an emotion associated with "a negative disposition, attitude or feeling," prompted by suspicions of "fear, rivalry, unfaithfulness" or anticipated loss of something of great personal value. (Dictionary.com, LLC, 2016). It often consists of a combination of emotions such as anger, resentment, inadequacy, helplessness, and disgust. Since scientists do not have a universally agreed upon definition of jealousy, it has been defined in a myriad of ways:

"Romantic jealousy is here defined as a complex of thoughts, feelings, and actions which follow threats to self-esteem and/or threats to the existence or quality of the relationship, when those threats are generated by the perception of a real or potential attraction between one's partner and a (perhaps imaginary) rival." (White, 1981, p. 24).

"Jealousy, then, is any aversive reaction that occurs as the result of a partner's extra dyadic relationship that is real, imagined, or considered likely to occur." (Bringle & Buunk, 1991, p. 135).

"Jealousy is conceptualized as a cognitive, emotional, and behavioral response to a relationship threat. In the case of sexual jealousy, this threat emanates from knowing or suspecting that one's partner has had (or desires to have) sexual activity with a third party. In the case of emotional jealousy, an individual feels threatened by her or his partner's emotional involvement with and/or love for a third party." (Guerrero, et al., 2004, p. 311).

"Jealousy is defined as a protective reaction to a perceived threat to a valued relationship, arising from a situation in which the partner's involvement with an activity and/or another person is contrary to the jealous person's definition of their relationship." (Breva, 2004, p. 195).

"Jealousy is triggered by the threat of separation from, or loss of, a romantic partner, when that threat is attributed to the possibility of the partner's romantic interest in another person." (Sharpteen & Kirkpatrick, 1997, p. 628).

I cannot attest to the fact that all the descriptions above are absolute in truth when it comes to defining jealousy. However, I can attest to the fact that I have experienced my own share of personal insecurities, inadequate feelings and introverted shortcomings as it relates to jealousy. Case in point: When it comes to my wife, there are a number of men who I trust to drive my wife from Miami to Maine without a second thought. By the same token, there are also one or two men who I would not trust to walk her to the mailbox. Of course, my perspectives have absolutely nothing to do with my wife or the integrity of these other men, but rather with my own false sense of insecurity and personal anxiety. My point is this: Jealousy can rear its ugly head at any time and at the most inopportune times. When it does, the outcome can be divisive in separating you from the person you supposedly love.

What then is the cause behind "hiding and hurting" men not being able to keep this "green-eyed monster" from raising its ugly head? I think the answer lies in what is alluded to but not directly stated in the previous descriptions of jealousy. That is, the issue of men not being able to "control" all the relationships in their lives. Most men will deny this fact but whenever they find themselves in a situation that magnifies their vulnerabilities, those vulnerabilities get projected onto someone else. That someone else is usually their spouse or significant other. Unfortunately, men often live by a different code of ethics than what is expected or required of their relational partner. They know how to comfortably dish it out but they are not comfortable receiving the same treatment in return. Men often excuse their actions by insisting that "it's a man thing." But what does that mean exactly? The best way to answer this question is to take a look at the creation of man; and when, where and how he made the mistake of believing this lie in the first place.

Root Cause of Jealousy

Adam was created by the Triune God (God the Father, God the Son, and God the Holy Spirit) and is the earthly replica of a divine imagination. With divine imagination came a plethora of positive, productive and "assigned" privileges: "And God said, Let us make man in our image, after our likeness: and let them have dominion over the fish of the sea, and over the fowl of the air, and over the cattle, and over all the earth, and over every creeping thing that creepeth upon the earth." (Genesis 1:26). Then came the icing on the cake, so to speak: "And God blessed them, and God said unto them, be fruitful, and multiply, and replenish the ear, and subdue it: and have dominion over the fish of the sea, and over the fowl of the air, and over every living thing that moveth upon the earth." (Genesis 1:28).

If I were to give psychological credence to these passages, I would surmise that men view themselves in light of their persona and identity with Adam, the first man. In other words, they view themselves first before everyone else and as the "number one man" among all men. But notice, God did not say, "Let us make MEN in our image" but rather "Let us make MAN in our image." (Genesis 1:26a). What this tells us is that God created the first man to serve as a reflection of Him; and not that man should dominate over others merely because he was created first. Because most men believe they were created first, they believe they were meant to be first (number one) in the relationship, and all others secondary. The root of this mindset lies in the spirit of jealousy—a jealousy birthed out of a thwarted and corrupt sense of dominance and entitlement. Moreover, there is also strong indication that the "sin" of jealousy was dormant (Genesis 1-3) until it reared its ugly head (Genesis 4), ultimately leading Cain to kill his brother Abel. (Genesis 4:1-10).

Sovereign Jealousy vs. Human Jealousy

In Exodus 34:14, the Lord God declares His "name is Jealous" and that He "is a jealous God" (Exodus

34:14). Is God in His eminent righteousness taking on an unholy attribute and name? Absolutely not. Then where did this ill-begotten seed of emotions stem from? Well, if you consider God's sovereignty then you understand that He has earned the right to define and call Himself jealous—not in humanistic terms but as a descriptive attribute of His divine persona. Human beings, especially men, cannot compare to the righteousness and sovereignty of God. Men who allow themselves to be lured into improper behavior and acts of jealousy are not reflecting the nature and behavior of God. Whenever the "green-eyed monster" of jealousy attacks us personally and privately, it causes us to attack others painfully and publicly.

Three Forms of Jealousy

Jealousy attacks men in ways that they are not prepared to handle. To understand how these attacks occur, let us explore them from three major perspectives: *Jealousy Attacks Men Intellectually.* The intellect is a faculty of reasoning, understanding and mental faculties. All of these actions (behaviors) are mentally driven, assessed and derived in the mind. As such, the intellect is also the seat of the *soul*. Understanding this should provide men with a deeper understanding of the degree to which jealousy ensues, attacks and plagues us. It can cause us to act without conscious thought or rationale. It can lead us down a path of shame and embarrassment. And it can create emotional outbursts that cause us to lash out against the people we love and care for or feel threatened by. Although everything inside us tells us to act to the contrary, when a man's intellect is attacked by jealousy, it causes him to act out in ways that he never imagined. By the time reality sets in and he grapples with how foolish he has been his character has been diminished. And the "green-eyed monster" who initiated this chain of events is nowhere to be found, to repair the damage done to others and his soul. At this point, the cost of forgiveness is overshadowed by an experience that is not easily forgotten. Why? Because once jealousy attacks, gaining access to a man's intellect it will find its way back to that place to repeat the process over and over again.

Jealousy Attacks Men Intuitively. Intuition is a cognitive process involving "a feeling that guides a person to act a certain way without fully understanding why." (Merrian-Webster.com, 2015-b). When a man's emotions are attacked by jealousy, it not only damages him in the moment but in the future as well. Although most men will never admit it, jealousy can plague a man's mind with a high degree of suspicion, simply because he obtains and stores knowledge in an ill-mannered fashion. Nothing is more damaging to a healthy relationship than a lack of trust at the intuitive level. It can create imaginative scenarios in a person's mind, involving obsessions and fixations that are not supported or sanctioned by reality.

In my many years of counseling in the secular and religious fields, I have seen a great deal of physical and emotional harm done to innocent people who are caught up in a whirlwind of confusion caused by corrupt intuition. Jealousy on the intuitive level can be a very destructive mechanism and tool for chaos. Everyone associated with it generally wants to distance themselves from the person exhibiting these qualities. Even worse, the man who is caught in the trap of jealousy is too blind to see himself and his actions for whom and what it truly is. It is almost as if men who operate in this manner acquire a sense of entitlement based on false intuition. Not only is it a very sad and ugly way to live but it is even worse to die this way.

Jealousy Attacks Men Creatively. Jealousy not only attacks the intellect and intuition but it also attacks a man's creativity and ability to inspire. Inspiration is a product of creative thinking. A man's ability to think creatively is what helps him to solve problems. When jealousy attacks a man's creative genius and inspirational process it causes relational problems with everyone he is involved with. Once the source of inspiration is corrupted, it causes a man to enter into a relational separation of himself from the source of his creativity.

We cannot disregard the fact that God created us to be earthly replicas of His divine imagination. If God's inspiration created us and dwells in us, then that same inspiration should be the driving force behind our creativity and holistic approach towards others. A man cannot afford to allow jealousy to invade his area of creative thought because it will affect every area of his life. Inspiration is meant to develop a man's character and creative purpose. But when it is thwarted by jealousy, it forces him to live beneath his privilege and God-given purpose. This limits his ability to be inspired and think creatively in difficult times.

The hidden hurt man will often camouflage his manhood against the backdrop of his manly deeds. Those of us who come in contact with him will likely never appreciate his value because the "green-eyed monster" of jealousy has infiltrated his mind, heart and world. Unless and until the hidden hurt man understands how it effects, he will never truly know how to overcome it. Instead, he will become a destructive platter to himself and anyone else that he expresses jealous emotions to. No matter how hard we try, jealousy is one of the few things that we simply cannot keep hidden.

CHAPTER: 4
BOYS NIGHT OUT

We all look for people of common interest to develop a bond and fellowship with. However, when it comes to the "boys night out"—that fraternal-like setting where men get together for food, drinks and to watch their favorite sports team on television—it can also be a place where hidden hurting men begin to spiral downward into a sea of loneliness and frustration. No matter how close a man may be to the boys at the table, needing (wanting) to expose your vulnerabilities to other men is a difficult thing for most men. To put things into perspective, let us compare a typical "boys night out" versus a "girls night out."

A Comparative Study: "Girl's Night Out"

Imagine there are four women who are close friends. One of the women confesses that she has been struggling with a personal challenge and feels the need to finally "let the cat out of the bag." She confesses to the other women that she is involved in a lesbian relationship and no longer wants to hide. After the initial shock, her friends offer moral support by initiating the following steps:

First, they try and convince her that her feelings may not be real. They offer caring and compassionate questions like: "What happened?", "Who is this other woman?" and "How long have you been feeling this way?" Rather than condemning her, her friends rally around her, enveloping her with their love, comfort and affection. Because they genuinely care for her, her secret did not cause a breach in their bond of "sisterhood" and, if need be, they are willing to sit with her until the restaurant closes.

Secondly, her friends begin to explore and discuss the downfalls of her heterosexual relationships and what motivated her to a change in lifestyle. They recognize that she has been possibly wounded, hurt, let down, abused and mistreated by the men in her life; and therefore, objectifies the men in her life as meaningless and no good. Despite her endless ranting against men, her friends listen intently with deep compassion, sympathy, empathy, and concern. They begin to encourage her by sharing some of their own personal stories and experiences to provide her with some alternative perspectives with respect to relationships.

Finally, her friends allow her to voice her concerns and all the reasons that brought her to this resolve. Despite of the fact that all three women confess that they do not share her passions and interest, and wish that she would reconsider the heterosexual lifestyle, they nonetheless pledge their support and unwavering love and friendship to her. She is strengthened by their resolve, which liberates her from the shame and ridicule of the experience. Though the possibility exists that her friends may discuss the matter in private, she is assured that their friendship is strong and their bond to each other is intact. As a result, they leave the table closer than when they arrived because that is the nature of a typical "girls night out."

The HIDDEN HURT Man

A Comparative Study: "Boys Night Out"

Now, let us play out the same scenario with four male friends. Similarly, during one of their usual gatherings one of the men confesses that he has been struggling with a particular challenge and feels the need to "let the cat out of the bag." After the initial shock, his friends take the following approach:

First, stunned beyond belief, his friends become visibly angry. They feel betrayed by him because of his secret, as they recant all the numerous times they patted each other on the rear end while playing basketball. The sheer thought of their friends preferred lifestyle sickens them to their stomach. Questions swirl in their minds: "Oh God, what if he has the HIV virus? Who is this guy he is involved with? What if it is someone we know?" Each of them contemplates asking the waiter for a box to go.

Secondly, against their better judgment, they decided to give their friend the benefit of the doubt by allowing him to express his feelings and explain his struggles. They begin to tune him out, not wanting to hear or initiate conversations that might lead to specific details. The very thought of his preferred lifestyle goes against every fiber of their macho image. It is clear that the conversation is becoming increasingly strained. One of the men secretly plays out a scenario of him punching his friend in the face to knock some sense into him. He smirks at the possibility of knocking his friend in a temporary state of unconsciousness and leaving him lying on the restaurant floor to suffer further humiliation from onlookers. Instead of compassion and care, the three men return cold glassy stares of condemnation and disgust.

Finally, as the three disloyal friends decide to end the gathering early, they take no thought for the hidden hurting man they are leaving behind. They make a point of reminding him repeatedly that the friendship is over and stained beyond repair. After all, how can they face him, each other and other men knowing that this guy is openly gay? If they maintain the relationship, they run the risk of being labeled with him. The once vibrant person who was a member of a collective group of friends is now broken and wounded. All that is left is a shell of a hidden hurting man, who realizes that he may never emotionally recover from the "boys' night out."

A Man's Competitive Nature

In real life, either of the two comparisons may or may not happen. They are merely possibilities of what could (might happen) to hidden hurting men. What we do know with great certainty is that a woman's approach during a "girl's night out" is likely to be considerably different from a man's approach during a "boys night out." The one lesson we can derive from both experiences is that there is a price to pay for being different.

Even if the events had nothing to do with the revealing of a hidden secret, the truth of the matter is men struggle when it comes to their relationships with other men. This is largely due to the competitive nature in men—what was defined in the last chapter as "men viewing themselves in light of their persona and identity with Adam, the first man." In other words, men viewing themselves first before everyone else, as the "number one man" among all men." *See* pg. 23. Most men, if they are honest, admit that they are driven by a spirit of competition at most male gatherings; what the old folks use to call, "pissing around the fire hydrant; or what I refer to as the "alpha dog syndrome."

The term, "alpha dog" refers to the lead authority among a group of like-minded friends. What is rarely understood when it comes to a "boy's night out" is this: When you bring four or more men together in one setting, who share similar gifts, talents, educational backgrounds and interests, there is bound to be competition. Only one will walk away as victor of the spoils. Consequently, there are at least five things that are evident at any male gathering:

(1) The Spirit of Competition – Somewhere during the course of social conversation, a number of conversational themes will be brought up—all subconsciously at first—with the goal of becoming the main topic of discussion. Generally speaking, whoever comes up with the best topic for discussion usually takes the lead in discussion. Regardless of how many other subjects are brought the discussion generally reverts back to the primary topic. Similar to the list of plays in a coach's playbook on game day, competitive men have a mental playbook recorded in their minds and are not easily persuaded to succumb to another man's desire to rule the conversation.

(2) The Reporting of Accomplishments – I cannot remember the last time I sat among my colleagues and friends, and there was no mention of our various accomplishments. It has been my experience that most men will not sit with their friends and colleagues if they do not have anything worthwhile to report. They must

have something to share, even if it is nothing more than a dream or fixation of their imagination. Since most of my friends and colleagues are ministers or pastors, it is virtually impossible to leave the table without hearing or sharing a plethora of sermons from those in attendance. The mere mention of a passage of scripture and we will all chime in on how we would approached the same text. And, of course, the amount of souls that came to the altar after the sermon is a good indication as to who had the best sermon at the table. Because of the raving popularity associated with social media sites, we no longer have to wait on our next physical gathering. That is, not when our fellow comrades can see us on Facebook "Live." All of this adds to our desire to have the greatest of accomplishments.

(3) The Plague of Prowess – I recognize that I may be revealing too much to the women who read this book but the "plague of prowess" is virtually discussed at every gathering, even when the other topics are not. According to Merriam-Webster Dictionary (2015-c), *prowess* has to do with "a superior skill you learn by study, practice or observation." There is rarely a time when a real man does not look for that one opportunity to show his mastery of a particular subject matter or thought. This superior skill is what causes a man to stand out among his peers, to be successful in his career and be admired by the opposite sex. It is the basis behind pastors asking each other, "How many members do you have at your church?" It is the basis behind business men asking each other, "What's in your portfolio?" And it is the basis of authors asking each other, "How many books have you written? How many guest lectures have you been invited to as a result of your work?" And yes, surprisingly, there is often enough

testosterone among the men at one gathering to match the wealth of King Solomon!

(4) The Next Bright Idea or Vision – God forbid if a group of men should sit at a table and not be able to share what we consider to be the "next best thing to sliced bread." It is the one thing that makes us great even if we have not accomplished anything in a few years. There is always some sad story or indictment against someone who missed out on an initial investment (i.e., Google, Apple, capital gains, etc.). If a man knows of something that is remotely considered to be of great value in the future, then he has secured a seat at the table among his colleagues and additional invitations will follow.

(5) Our Manhood at Home – Please do not get it twisted. In the one to three hours of dialogue among men, the one question that always comes up is: How's it going at home? From the beginning of time (or at least since I was born in 1963) there has been the familiar saying that a man should be the "king of his castle." It has even been suggested in modern times that a man needs a personal "man cave" within the castle he rules over. One of the prerequisites required of a man—to be invited to the table with his colleagues and friends—is that he is the authority in his household. Even though most men are tired, they will continue to hang out with their friends just to prove that they are not bound to the rules of a curfew or the "lady of the house." And woe unto the man who constantly receives calls, tweets, texts or Facebook messages to come home. This man may never (ever) live such an occasion down in the eyes of his peers!

Imagine the frustration a man must feel trying to survive when he is weakened by his own personal dilemmas. Being plagued with the titles of "alpha dog" and "king of the castle" while bearing the weight of his hidden vulnerabilities. Imagine what it must feel like as man when he knows all too well that it is tough enough trying to survive when you are emotionally healthy, let alone when you are emotionally wounded. How does he bear up to his responsibilities when everyday life continues to chip away at his core?

Occasionally, I am fortunate enough to catch one of the documentaries on television, involving the survival techniques of animals. It is quite interesting to watch how an animal can conjure up the courage to fight another up and coming male leader within his group. The same competitive fight exists in every man—whether he wants to admit it or not and regardless of his sentiments towards other males within his circle of friends. There is always a fight to get to the top and an even greater fight to remain at the top.

"Boys Night Out," at its best, allows each man gathered at the table to know where he stands amongst his peers. The reality for most men is, if you cannot win at the table with your peers, then how can you win on a larger scale with your competitors. This reality reminds me of a favorite Bible passage that challenges us to never measure yourself according to the score at the table: "If thou has run with the footmen, and they have wearied thee, then how canst thou contend with horses? And if in the land of peace, wherein thou trusted, they wearied thee, then how wilt thou do in the swelling of the Jordan? (Jeremiah 12:5)

CHAPTER: 5
THE GOD FACTOR

Inevitably at some point we have to talk about God. Christians assert that God is an automatic "cure all" for any problem or situation and to be perfectly honest they are right. However, in light of the title and overall theme of this book—*The Hidden Hurt Man*—God is not always the first option for men who are hidden and hurting. If I can be transparent, it took me well over six months to write this chapter. The reason it took me so long is because I had accepted a new pastoral position at New Mt. Zion Missionary Baptist Church in Daytona Beach, Florida in January 2014. The first half of that year was a period of adjustment with regards to new ministerial assignments. But the second reason and most honest reason of all had to do with God's influence in my life. This is what I mean when I refer to the "God factor." Due to my strongly held beliefs as a Christian, it was difficult to write this chapter because I had to write it from a male perspective, keeping in mind all the men who have never known or experienced God or Jesus Christ as Savior and Lord. I finally reached the conclusion that this chapter will probably not offer many solutions for the hidden hurt man; but it can serve as a means of oral arguments to explain why some men remain hidden and hurting, in spite of who they are and what they believe. If nothing else, my prayer is that it will be a source of strength and help to them. Therefore, I offer three arguments to the hidden hurt man who wants to desperately escape the burdensome guilt of needing to hide because of unresolved hurt:

Argument #1: "The Missing Father Syndrome"

Somewhere around the mid-1980's, the *Single Parent Era* began to change the dynamics of the family structure. Sadly, in these ever changing social times little has changed. Kirsten Andersen of *Life Site News* stated:

> "Today, one-third of American children—a total of 15 million—are being raised without a father. Nearly five million more children live without a mother. Children without fathers are much more likely to grow up in poverty. While married couples with children enjoy an average income of $80,000, single mothers average only $24,000. Though poverty is the primary risk factor for fatherlessness, absenteeism among fathers has also been overwhelmingly a black problem, regardless of poverty status, reports the Times. The majority of black children nationwide – 54 percent – are being raised by single mothers. Only 12 percent of black families below the poverty line have both parents present, compared with 41 percent of poor Hispanic families and 32 percent of poor white families. In all but eleven states, most black children do not live with both parents. In every state, 70 percent of white children do. In all but two states, most Hispanic children do." (Andersen, 2015).

There are a number of men, particularly African-Americans (ages 25-40), who have never had a father figure to trust in or rely on. As such, when God the Father is presented as an alternative option to fulfill the role of father in a man's life, it immediately raises suspicion. Building trust in a man who is already hurting can present a series of challenges. For one, the principles needed to establish trust in a relationship, such as love, interaction, hope, faith, etc., the concept is a foreign one because they are non-existent. Here is where the concept of relationship and fatherhood loses ground from a biblical perspective:

> "And God said, Let us make man in our image, after our likeness: and let them have dominion over the fish of the sea, and over the fowl of the air, and over the cattle, and over all the earth, and over every creeping thing that creepeth upon the earth." (Genesis 1:26).

Trust is one of the greatest and most difficult challenges a man can face. It is far easier for a man to release and let go of any false hopes of fatherhood than to live with the expectation of a father who is visibly absent. In the mind of a man who is hurting, there is no basis for trusting a heavenly Father when his earthly father (who supposedly was created in the image and likeness of God) failed to set an example. His rationale is reduced to a simple question. That is, why believe in either (Heavenly Father vs. earthly father) when both are visibly absent and not real? Trusting and waiting on God to manifest Himself to a man already in crisis merely enhances a man's urgency to stay clear of any potential disappointments or let downs. Besides, being alone is far more convenient, soothing and settling to a man's psyche as opposed to feeling abandoned and alone. With that said, I offer the following acronym pertaining to TRUST as a model for building trust in the hidden hurt man:

T (TASTES) – Trust cannot be established if there is no similarity in tastes. This does not mean, of course, that men are to like the same sports team. But it does mean having an equal regard and respect for each other, as well as each other's opinions. Here is an example of what I mean: One of my closest friends formerly played professional baseball for the Los Angeles Dodgers but my passion and preferred sport was basketball. Regardless of the circumstances, I always made it a point to keeping up with the Dodgers because I knew my friend and I would eventually have a conversation about it. Similarly, my friend also made a point of keeping up with the Miami Heat for my sake, even though we both knew that LeBron James had returned to Cleveland.

R (RITUALS) – Trust cannot be established without the rituals of manhood. To a man, there are basic beliefs that all men agree on without arguing. Some of these ritualistic expressions include statements like: "There is nothing more astonishing than a beautiful woman," "Money answers all problems" and "Silence is golden."

U (UNIFICATION) – Trust cannot be established if we fail to unite in a mutual cause. At some point in a man's partnership with his friends, he must be willing to stand in support of their cause, with the hope that one day they will stand in support of your cause in return.

S (SUMMONS) – Trust cannot be established without the intrusion of one's sacrifice and time on behalf of a friend. A man must be willing to give of himself, even if his giving imposes upon his time and personal space.

T (TERRITORY) – Trust cannot be established if there is no willingness to share sacred interests and possessions of trust. This includes but is not limited to the things a man specializes in such as his talents, gifts and calling.

So, as you can see, the God factor can be an extremely difficult concept for the hidden hurt man to accept because he is not willing to commit (in full surrender) to many of the relational attributes above. If there is no mutual agreement between the two, then it precludes any possibility of God building a healthy Father-son relationship with a man who is afflicted and haunted by the absenteeism of an earthly father.

Argument #2: "The Preacher Perception"

The "preacher perception" stems from a widely held cultural and religious perspective of the African American Church Culture. The perspective revolves around a distrust and personal complex for pastors (preachers) in the church. It would be so easy to skip past the details of this issue and simply regard it as a "black thing" but that would not bring clarity to the argument. The real issue here for the Black male is a matter of control and trust. That is, he distrusts any pastor (preacher) in the church who appears to have a greater influence over his wife, girlfriend or significant other;

particularly, if he is not a member and senses a loss of control. Let me explain what I mean by this in greater detail.

Faith and religion in their purest form is a matter of choice and the heart. The Bible says, "Keep and guard your heart with all vigilance and above all that you guard, for out of it flow the springs of life." (Proverbs 4:23, AMP). It is the condition of the heart then that determines one's quality of life and capacity to love, have joy, peace, comfort, confidence, etc. The heart "knows" and "reacts" based on what it hears and as a result of what is spoken or poured into it. Moreover, God created man to serve as a spokesman of life and to serve as a protector to his wife and family. The story of Adam and Eve is a prime example of what can occur when a man fails to "speak and protect" against the influence of wrong thinking, wrong dialogue, wrong influences and wrong input of knowledge and information for the wrong sources:

> "Now the serpent was more subtle than any beast of the field which the Lord God had made. And he said unto the woman, Yea, hath God said, Ye shall not eat of every tree of the garden? And the woman said unto the serpent, We may eat of the fruit of the trees of the garden: But of the fruit of the tree which is in the midst of the garden, God hath said, Ye shall not eat of it, neither shall ye touch it, lest ye die. And the serpent said unto the woman, Ye shall not surely die: For God doth know that in the day ye eat thereof, then your eyes shall be opened, and ye shall be as gods,

knowing good and evil. And when the woman saw that the tree was good for food, and that it was pleasant to the eyes, and a tree to be desired to make one wise, she took of the fruit thereof, and did eat, and gave also unto her husband with her; and he did eat." (Gen. 3:1-6).

As is the case with most African-American men, hidden hurting men often feel threatened when their woman speaks too fondly or favorably about another man. Although her actions, more often than not, are perfectly innocent, the mere sharing of it raises concerns in the man because he did not initiate it. Women often derive strength from what is spoken from the pulpit but their exuberance in wanting to share it often comes across as a betrayal of her intimacy and relationship with her man. Since hidden hurt men often have unresolved issues and suffer from a personal private pain of their own, they perceive any change in a woman's spiritual development and enthusiasm as a personal threat to his role as spokesman and protector. In turn, the man interprets the voice of the pastor (preacher) as a threat because he believes he is losing her as a result of the pastors (preachers') influence. A man's disdain for the church then is premised on his dislike and distrust of the pastor (preacher) who he believes is competing with him for his family and home, which of course is rarely the case.

What a lot of men do not realize is that most women long for men to assume their role as the primary spokesperson and protector of their lives. They long for him to speak good things, positive things, sweet things, encouraging things or anything that is not harmful, demeaning or degrading. And to many a man's surprise, a woman is particularly interested in hearing about the pains of her man and will do almost anything in her power to support him. But this too is a hard reality for most hidden hurt men to understand.

So, once again, the God factor is a crippling concept for the hidden hurting man due to his false perceptions of the pastor (preacher), church and perceived threats to his woman.

Argument #3: "The Sensitive Worshipper"

Over the past twenty years there has been a major shift in the perceived image of those who lead worship in the church. When I grew up as a teenager over thirty-five years ago, the men who served on the praise team and in the choir were also actively involved in sports—basketball, football, baseball, track and field, etc. However, in this present day, there appears to be a more effeminate nature to some of the male worshipers and most do not play any type of sports. The conclusion is that church has been infiltrated by a "softer" type of man. And as previously discussed in the chapter, *Boys Night Out*, this is unacceptable behavior.

Another concern relates to the leadership of the church. An increasing number of churches are now being led by women; who by reason of their gender are perceived as having contributed to this tendency towards femininity. With the absence of a major father figure in the home and the insertion of women in roles of leadership, vast numbers of men in the church are no longer viewed in the same light as the tough rugged men of the past. And let us not forget the influence and scandalous actions of pastors (priests) who molest and take advantage of young boys, who look up to them as a father figure. The prevailing issues stemming from the church fosters an ongoing resentment in the mind of the hidden hurting man.

A man's inability to find safety and refuge in the church translates as not finding a man that he can identify with. Consequently, as it relates to the God factor, a man feels justified in remaining hidden to avoid exposing all the pain and hurt he is feeling and sensing. In his mind, the God who can help, will not or cannot help because He is not accessible and therefore absent in his life. These are but a few of the hindrances associated with the God factor.

CHAPTER: 6
THE CURSE OF IMPOTENCY

"Now there is at Jerusalem by the sheep market a pool, which is called in the Hebrew tongue Bethesda, having five porches. In these lay a great multitude of impotent folk, of blind, halt, withered, waiting for the moving of the water." (John 5:2-3).

A man's greatest fear is IMPOTENCY. The season of life when a man "lacks power, strength and vigor" and/or experiences feelings of "helplessness" associated with ungovernable inadequacies." (Merriam-Webster, Inc., 2015-d). Whether a man is grounded in Christian principles or merely a sojourner traveling through the confusing maze of life, every man needs (wants) to be potent (powerful) and strong. And rightfully so, since the desire was given to him at creation by a Creator who spoke blessings upon him and his woman to be fruitful, multiply, replenish, subdue and have dominion over the rest of God's created works. (Genesis 1:26-28). When a man no longer feels powerful and strong but instead feels impotent, he will hide himself to camouflage the hurt he is feeling.

The medical profession links "impotency" with a man's sexual prowess and/or inability to "engage in sexual intercourse [due to] the inability to have and maintain an erection." (TheFreeDictionary.com, 2003-2016). Physicians diagnose this as "erectile dysfunction." But when impotency is associated with a man's aura—an unseen emanation surrounding the body—it can be detrimental to his survival. Consider, for example, the word "impotency" and its use. It is never used to describe a woman's inability to be a woman. And yet, tragically, it is used as an indictment against the male psyche.

It is believed that the selling of Viagra, Cialis and Levitra has become billion-dollar business. To their shame, companies have profited off the backs of men who are deemed sexually impotent. However, in the context of a man's feelings of helplessness and inadequacies, impotency can also have physical and spiritual consequences. The Gospel of John offers five "figurative" reasons for a man experiences a season of impotency. (John 5:3). Out of the five, three are worth mentioning:

(1) Blindness – *Blindness* is equated to an "inability to see; unable to notice or judge something; accepting the actions or decisions of someone or something without any questions or criticism." (Merriam-Webster, Inc., 2015-e). Figuratively speaking, when a man is plagued with blindness it causes him great uncertainty as it relates to his next step or move in life. If he is imprisoned by his emotions—plagued by fear, frustration, disappointment and anger—he will not be overly anxious or eager to ask for help. He is not only emotionally blinded by his surroundings but his blindness impairs his ability to see fully his potential and how to avoid to maneuver in spite of his blindness. In the hands of blindness, a hidden hurting man becomes a diminished version of himself.

(2) Halt – *Halt* is attributed to someone who is "considered as lame, having an injured leg or foot that makes walking difficult or painful; not strong, good, or

effective; not smart or impressive." (Merriam-Webster, Inc., 2015-f). Men have systematically been indoctrinated by a society that demands that men have a form of "swagger" (or "swag" as the modern day youth call it) about them. But how can a hidden hurting man walk with an undaunted level of confidence when his inward man is crippled emotionally? Some horrific experience from his past or some current event may have induced a sort of castration that has deprived him of the vitality of his manhood. Or something could have affected him psychologically, leaving him afraid of taking another chance to overcome his plight.

(3) Withered – *Withered* implies "to become dry and sapless; to shrivel from as if from loss of bodily moisture; to lose vitality, force, or freshness; or to make speechless or incapable of action." (Merriam-Webster, Inc., 2015-g). To be emotionally blind and lame (halt) is one thing but to be emotionally withered is far worse. To be "withered" suggests that there was once life and vibrancy but now there is lifelessness and a depletion of life. On occasion, we hear of stories where someone came into extraordinary riches and wealth, only to end up a few years later in a place of destitution and poverty because of their inability to manage and maintain prosperity. The same holds true when it comes to an emotionally withered man, who for a period of time lived in abundance but now is living beneath his privilege.

Defining these three figurative causes is only a part of the battle. The question that arises is: how does a man find himself lured into a state of impotency? Knowing that no man (in his right mind) wants to find himself in this state of being, it is imperative that we identify some of the causes in order to plan our escape from its grasp. So let's go back and further investigate these three figurative causes, to see if we can pull some hidden hurt man out of the abyss of his dilemma.

Blindness

In an article published by Everyday Health entitled, "What Causes Blindness," Dennis Thompson, Jr. insisted that "normal vision depends on a multi-faceted, complex process. Light enters the eye through the cornea and lens, with the iris helping to focus the image. The light is projected onto the back wall of the eye, where it is perceived by millions of tiny nerve endings that make up the retina. From here, the retina translates the images into nerve impulses that are transmitted to the brain through the optic nerve." (Thompson, 2010). Stated simply, when any part of the eye is damaged, either through illness or injury, blindness can occur:

The lens may cloud, obscuring the light entering the eye.

The eye's shape can change, altering the image projected onto the retina.

The retina can degrade and deteriorate, affecting the perception of images.

The optic nerve can become damaged, interrupting the flow of visual information to the brain.
What is the cause of a hidden hurt man's emotional blindness? And what prevents him from seeing as he

should? A clue to these questions might lie in an evaluation of the lens, eye shape, retina, and optic nerve: The Lens – When I think of the lens of the eye—the clear part of the eye that focuses light to form clear images—I equate it to the emotional state of a man's "apathy of perception." One of the great causes of a hidden hurt man's imprisonment into emotional doom is his inability to express his emotions in a positive way. For him, life has become a horrific display of constant disappointments from others, as well as from himself. Having constantly viewed his life as a struggle of "no way outs," preceded by a constant denial of "no way ins," resulting from those who refuse to lend a helping hand. As a result of not seeing any light at the end of the tunnel, he ultimately chooses to remain in this state of hopeless despair.

Eye Shape – When I think of the shape of the eye, I equate it to the emotional state and "analysis of a man's personality." Hosea 4:6 says, "My people are destroyed for lack of knowledge: because thou hast rejected knowledge, I will also reject thee…" When a hidden hurt man is incapable of figuring out what defines his personality, he may be forever doomed to covering up his character imperfections. And thus, he is continuously left standing outside the doors of opportunity that is afforded to those who know themselves well. Moreover, how can others be of assistance in helping him when he does not even know how to help himself?

The Retina – When I think of the retina (the sensitive tissue at the back of the eye that receives images and sends signals to the brain) and how it relates to the emotional state of the hidden hurt man, I think of the absence of polarity. The word polarity means, "a state in which two ideas, opinions, etc., are completely opposite or very different from each other." (Merriam-Webster, Inc., 2015-h). In relation to the hidden hurt man it implies not being able to adequately and effectively decipher your most recent encounters. The old folks used to say it this way: "You wouldn't know a good thing if it were staring you right in the face." Men who are guilty of "absence of polarity" are often hurting the ones who love them the most and loving the ones who could care less about them. They are often plagued by a sense of entitlement and are guilty of literally driving away those who genuinely care about them. And all because they do not know how to decipher between the good, bad, and ugly, and place them in their perspective categories for their own benefit. When you believe that you are not good to/for yourself, then how can you be expected to be good to/for someone else?

The Optic Nerve – When I think of what the optic nerve (the pair of cranial nerves that pass from the retina to the optic chiasm and conduct visual stimuli to the brain) and what it could represent in relation to the emotional state of a hidden hurt man, I think of the "agony of personification." This is probably the worst state that a man can be in compared to the previous three (i.e., the lens, eye shape and retina) mentioned in this chapter. To be overwhelmed by the agony of personification is to suggest that we are out of step with ourselves. It is like a person wishing that he were never born as opposed to taking responsibility for his own actions in contrast to his purpose. When this lot befalls a hidden hurt man, he becomes a menace to society and does everything he can to not be who God created him to be. Self-sabotage becomes a constant end to all of his beginnings. Those who are sucked into the vacuum of his self-inflicting personality are often hurt beyond repair as a result of the emotional abuse they encounter through him. It is a destructive behavior bent on pulling everyone around him down to his level. As the old folks use to say, "Misery loves company."

All four—the lens, eye shape, retina and optic nerve—contribute to the hidden hurt man's emotional blindness; creating a cursed season of impotency that cripples his drive and stride for becoming the man that God desires him to be.

Halt

Anything that grinds to a "halt" stops completely. Stopping completely, such that there is no growth, development or activity, is one of the greatest tragedies to befall a hidden hurt man. As God's greatest creation, the man and woman were blessed. God gave them the awesome mandate to be fruitful, multiply replenish, subdue, and have dominion over all things.

In spite of this great mandate, the hidden hurt man in no way resembles what God originally intended. It is as though, in succumbing to the pressures of life, his life suddenly "halted" and came to a complete stop. This state of morbid existence could literally push a man to feeling as if he is nothing and worth nothing. Since he has determined in his mind that he is doomed to be nothing, he gives up and decides he might as well do nothing. Now, imagine how this effects the lives of the people who have chosen to follow the image of this man? What happens to his sons when it comes to guidance? Or his daughter when it comes to protection? Or his wife when it comes to companionship? What becomes of them collectively when his "manhood" is silenced by his absenteeism? Or when he is reduced to a shell of manhood who is void of substance, procreative power and the ability to mold and encourage his family to become what God created them to be? What is it that stops a man's emotional growth?

Growth, in the physical sense, is caused by a healthy pituitary gland ("a pea-sized gland that sits at the base of the skull, underneath the brain and behind the bridge of the nose"). (Merriam-Webster, Inc., 2015-i). It senses the body's needs and sends signals to different organs and glands throughout the body to regulate their function and maintain an appropriate environment. Through the production of its hormones, the pituitary gland controls metabolism, growth, sexual maturation, reproduction, blood pressure and many other vital physical functions and processes.

Now, consider how this relates to the emotional growth of a hidden hurt man. Symbolically speaking, the "pituitary gland" would be equated to his "confidence and pride;" or that feeling of respect you have for yourself that garners respect from other people. When a man's level of confidence and pride is "firing on all cylinders," then everything around him will grow. And his emotions are providing the maximum amount of power to conquer any and all obstacles. By the same token, when a man's confidence level and pride is facing challenges of uncertainty and frailty, it can open him up to vulnerabilities that are detrimental to his productive growth. As it relates to his emotional development (which is often harder to pinpoint than his physical development), it increases self-awareness and self-regulation.

In an article entitled, *Social and Emotional Development*, an inference is made how the social skills and emotional development portrayed in PBS' *Sesame Street* aided in a child's ability to pay attention, transition from one activity to another and cooperate with others. These skills are crucial for early school preparedness. Also, in an article published by *Emotional Development* (Sept. 16, 2013), Teresa Odle stated: "Emotional development does not occur in isolation; neural, cognitive, and behavioral development interacts with emotional development and social and cultural influences and context also plays a role." (Odle, 2013).

How does this fair symbolically with the hidden hurt man? Well, whenever a man is unsure of the impactful role that his social and cultural influences are designed to play in his life, it can leave him "out of the loop" of things that are vital to his success. The inability to effectively interact with others leaves him feeling isolated and alone, which ultimately lures him back into a place of unresolved darkness.

Finally, when a hidden hurt man's activities are "halted," it is indicative of that season in life where (as the old folks use to say) "his get up and go, has gotten up and gone." Moreover, if we group a man's activities into the categories of "work" or "pleasure" and infuse his thinking with the notion that these things are designed to make him feel vigorous, energetic, and alive, he will in essence "feel like a man." But what happens when neither his work nor his desired pleasures are producing the anticipated results? What can suffice as an outlet to boost his ego and stimulate his heart's contentment? Where will he receive the applause of appreciation that motivates him to continue dreaming of bigger things and greater possibilities? A man halted in his activities becomes like a sink clogged with hair and guck. He functions but with great difficulty and a very slow process.

Withered

There is a very interesting story nestled in the Gospel of Mark 3:1-6 (AMP):

> "AGAIN JESUS went into a synagogue, and a man was there who had one withered hand [as the result of accident or disease]. And [the Pharisees] kept watching Jesus [closely] to see whether He would cure him on the Sabbath, so that they might get a charge to bring against Him [formally]. And He said to the man who had the withered hand, Get up [and stand here] in the midst. And He said to them, Is it lawful and right on the Sabbath to do good or to do evil, to save life or to take it? But they kept silence. And He glanced around at them with vexation and anger, grieved at the hardening of their hearts, and said to the man, Hold out your hand. He held it out, and his hand was [completely] restored. Then the Pharisees went out and immediately held a consultation with the Herodians against Him, how they might [devise some means to] put Him to death."

Although the story ends well for the man with the withered hand in that he gets healed and is able to function normally, there are a few things that also occur

The HIDDEN HURT Man

that can at times work against a man already hiding because of his hurt; or hurting because he has no choice but to hide. Observe the following mishaps associated with being withered:

First, there is the issue of the "accident", "incident", "disease" or "dilemma" that caused the man to be in a withered state in the first place. Unfortunately, hidden hurt men do not always get a chance to carry a sign with them stating what caused their predicament. As a result, they often face the scrutiny of other people's opinions, which leaves them feeling ostracized and wounded without proper cause. To be perfectly honest, most people are not even interested in your story. All they see is your withered condition and that is often enough for them to see you as "less than."

Secondly, there is the issue of other people's "issues" with someone else's response to your withered plight. What is obvious about the story above is the onlookers were more concerned about Jesus and whether they could catch Him in a compromising position, to further ridicule and persecute Him. The concerns of the man with the withered hand were irrelevant to them. The same can be said of the hidden hurt man in that they are often used as pawns to satisfy the judgmental schemes and scandals of someone else's underhanded and mischievous plot.

Thirdly, and probably the most challenging, is the moment when the hidden hurt man is placed on display in a room filled with men who appear normal. As if it is not already difficult enough to show up to a place that appears normal, imagine how a hidden hurt man feels when he is asked to stand in the presence of those who could care less about him and display his frailty and withered condition. So many hidden hurt men are pushed further into their hole of obscurity, based on the sad indictment that they are regarded as withered spectacles of insignificance.

Whether a hidden hurt man's impotency is caused by an emotional state of blindness, halt, or by reason of being withered, the desired outcome is the same: That there would be some means of escape into the dark dungeon of pain associated with his impotence. When will it come, how will it come, and whether it will set him free remains to be seen. For the hidden hurt man, impotency is no fun. And the lack of fun serves to further imprison him behind walls of fear, frustration, and fatalities. As the lyrics of a song I once wrote says:

> How long must I wait
> What more must I take
> Before You (God) shall come
> And the victory is won

CHAPTER: 7
I'M SICK OF DENZEL

Let us establish one thing from the start. There is a competitiveness that crumbles a man's character and it is not Denzel Washington, personally. Denzel is merely a symbol and metaphoric example of behavior. If this book were written in the 60's it could have easily been called, "I'm Sick of Sidney Poitier;" in the 70's, I'm Sick of Richard Roundtree;" in the 80's, "I'm Sick of Louis Gossett, Jr.;" or in the 90's, "I'm Sick of Blair Underwood." The greatest hindrance to a man who is hidden and hurting is *not* knowing how to bounce back from the pressures associated with his competitive nature. The pressures that cripple and at times castrate a man's character are brought on by the women in his life. Women like his wife, girlfriend, big sister, overly supportive mother, etc., who want to encourage him but often end up making him feel small and insignificant in relation to his manhood.

The problem with the "Denzel Syndrome" is it is based on an image created by a character in the plot of a movie that is not real. In one movie he reflects his sensitivity. In a second, he shows his strength. In a third, he displays what I define as his "stroft" (strong + soft) side. The challenge facing the hidden hurt man is he does not stand a chance with such an image looming over his head. As much as a man might want to please his woman, her appetite to see Denzel reflected in him is far too great of a task for him. Take for example, the following acronym and the struggle men face in trying to be like Denzel:

"D" (Dapper Effect)

One of the great challenges in trying to live up to the "Denzel Syndrome" is his suave image of perfection. Crossing every "t", dotting every "i" and pronouncing every "p" with an assertive pop is not easy but Denzel does it well. As such, pressure is placed on men to function as a social elite in all settings. When just showing up is a milestone in itself. Becoming dapper (neat and trim in appearance; spruce and stylish; alert and lively in movement and manners) is not just about clothes. It is a mindset centered on a positive image of self—an image that is not always easy and sometimes not even warranted. And yet this is the image most women desire in their man whether he can live up to it or not. Most men are not willing to discuss how they truly feel with their woman for fear of being rejected, neglected or even looking stupid. The woman in turn assumes that he just does not want to improve his quality of life. And in the solitude of his own mind he is probably screaming, "I'm Sick of Denzel!"

"E" (Electrifying Spirit)

"Thirty years after war turned the world into a wasteland, a lone warrior named Eli (starring Denzel Washington) marches across the ruined landscape, carrying hope for humanity's redemption. Only one other man (Gary Oldman) understands the power of what Eli carries, and he is determined to take it for himself. Though Eli prefers peace, he will risk death to protect his precious cargo, for he must fulfill his destiny to help restore mankind." (The Book of Eli, 2010).

The above words captured the essence of the story plot to the 2010 Action Thriller, *The Book of Eli*. Imagine the audience's response when they discover that Eli's book was the last copy of the Bible. To some Eli was a great protector. To others he was a menace to society. Eli's story reminds me of a similar story in the Bible:

> "And they came over unto the other side of the sea, into the country of the Gadarenes. And when he was come out of the ship, immediately there met him out of the tombs a man with an unclean spirit, Who had his dwelling among the tombs; and no man could bind him, no, not with chains: Because that he had been often bound with fetters and chains, and the chains had been plucked asunder by him, and the fetters broken in pieces: neither could any man tame him. And always, night and day, he was in the mountains, and in the tombs, crying, and cutting himself with stones. But when he saw Jesus afar off, he ran and worshipped him, And cried with a loud voice, and said, What have I to do with thee, Jesus, thou Son of the most high God? I adjure thee by God, that thou torment me not. For he said unto him, Come out of the man, thou unclean spirit. And he asked him, What is thy name? And he answered, saying, My name is Legion: for we are many. And he besought him

much that he would not send them away out of the country. Now there was there nigh unto the mountains a great herd of swine feeding. And all the devils besought him, saying, Send us into the swine, that we may enter into them. And forthwith Jesus gave them leave. And the unclean spirits went out, and entered into the swine: and the herd ran violently down a steep place into the sea, (they were about two thousand;) and were choked in the sea. And they that fed the swine fled, and told it in the city, and in the country. And they went out to see what it was that was done. And they come to Jesus, and see him that was possessed with the devil, and had the legion, sitting, and clothed, and in his right mind: and they were afraid." (Mark 5:1-15).

Sometimes the greatest hope of recovery and deliverance for a hidden hurt man is what he carries in his heart in relation to God. Maintaining this "electrifying spirit" can be a challenge for the hidden hurt man. Especially, when he is confronted by people who view him as a threat because of what he possesses in his heart. As in the case of Eli, it can be demanding to be both a personal support and savior to others, when you are struggling to maintain your own self-preservation. What does a hidden hurt man do when he is trying to define his own sense of divine purpose, while meeting the needs of everyone else's quirks? He screams, "I'm Sick of Denzel!"

"N" (Nemesis Nature of Narcissistic Neglect)

Narcissism (i.e., egoism and egocentrism) is a plaguing thought for the hidden hurt man. Add to this, the notion of narcissism becoming his "nemesis" (an enemy who is difficult to defeat) and there you will find an empty shell of a man. How can he be Denzel when he is guilty of neglecting his own will to be a man? Defined by the doctor's pronouncement and prompted by that "thing" dangling between his legs, he is regarded as fully developed. He is supposed to possess "swag" but offers no claim to have what it takes to woo every woman. Portrayed by an overwhelming confident strut, that pep in his step is not a confident swag but a limp from a former injury caused by an accidental fall down a flight of stairs at work. A fall, mind you, that he never reported for fear of losing his job if he dared apply for workers comp.

He is far from the smooth and suave Denzel character known as Bleak in the 1990 Spike Lee film, *Mo' Better Blues*. The character who is wooed by a sweet teacher called Indigo and a sultry singer called Clarke, while at the same time battling with a fellow band member and saxophonist called Shadow (Wesley Snipes). And no, the hidden hurt man is never guilty of narcissism even though it is a necessary character trait to compete in this dog-eat-dog world.

"Z" (Zeus Effect)

In Greek mythology the name Zeus is synonymous with being the most powerful of all the gods and yet guilty of a number of illicit affairs. One such affair involved Alcmene (wife of Amphityron), who bore Zeus a human -immortal son called Hercules. As a result of his frequent acts of infidelity, Zeus often caused friction between those seeking to be loyal to him.

R&B soul singer, Mary J. Blige, talks about the nature of bad boys and their infidelity in her song, *Mr. Wrong* (featuring Drake). Listen to the lyrics:

> *Bad boys ain't no good*
> *Good boys ain't no fun*
> *Lord knows that I should*
> *Run off with the right one*
> *Me and Mr. Wrong get along so good (so good)*
> *Even though he breaks my heart so bad (so bad)*
> *We got a special thing going on*
> *Me and Mr. Wrong (mister wrong)*
> *Even if I try, no, I never could*
> *Give him up cause his loves like that*
> *Ain't no way that I'm moving on*
> *I love my Mr. Wrong"*

To be perfectly honest, a hidden hurt man cannot measure up to this great lover in disguise. He is neither Zeus nor Mr. Wrong. And yet, that is exactly the character Denzel plays as Alonzo Harris in *Training Day*, with a god-like persona that suggests he can do no wrong. He is not bothered by all the wrong he does because (as he states in one of the scenes), "King Kong ain't got sh*t on me." (Training Day, 2001). Some women like a little "thug" in their man. But for a hidden hurt man, it can be a little threatening and intimidating to his own inner struggles. The very thought of having to play such a disturbing persona (merely for the pride and pleasure of his woman's fantasies) makes him want to shout out loud, "I'm Sick of Denzel!"

"E" (Eeriness of Expectations)

In the movie, *John Q.*, Denzel's character and story centers on a man whose nine-year-old son is in desperate need of a life-saving transplant. When he discovers that his medical insurance will not cover the costs of the surgery and alternative aid is not available, John Q. Archibald takes a hospital emergency room hostage in a last-ditch effort to save his child. Strangely, this is only after being verbally pushed by fear, anger, frustration and running out of options and ideas, as a result of the disparity of his wife, Denise (Kimberly Elise) who screams over the phone: "Do something John!" (John Q, 2002).

This is what I call the "eeriness of expectations" or what I consider to be the greatest fear of the hidden hurt man. He fears it because it forces him to act and respond in ways that go against logic. In context, I do not mean to imply that women are the downfall or trouble behind every hidden hurt man's dilemma because they most certainly are not. However, how a man sees himself through the eyes of his significant other (regardless of how casual the acquaintance) makes an indelible impression and impact on his life, actions and responses.

Living up to someone else's expectations are the equivalent of seeds planted into the heart and spirit of a person, for cultivation and development. In some respects, there is nothing wrong with that. Most men are the product of seeds of expectation planted by their parents and others who inspire greatness in them. However, most men are not taught how to handle disappointments, failure and the delays of life or to have a "Plan B" in place when things go awry. For some men, the process of discovery and insightful revelation is a better course of action for learning these things. For the hidden hurt man, the full scope of the learning process has not always been a favorable experience; and those who should be supporting him on his journey have left him to cry out in lonely frustration, "I'm Sick of Denzel".

"L" (Luxurious Leisure)

Who can ever forget the 2007 box office hit, *American Gangster*. A story based on the true life story of Frank Lucas (portrayed by Denzel Washington), who became a chauffeur for one of Harlem's leading mobsters. After his boss dies, Frank applies his own ingenuity and strict business code to become one of the inner city's most powerful crime bosses. Meanwhile, veteran cop, Richie Roberts (Russell Crowe) senses a change in the mob's power structure and looks for ways to bring his opponent to justice. This action packed film explores what it feels like to live a life of luxury and leisure, despite the erroneous methods use to accomplish that feat. And even though Frank Lucas eventually pays for his actions with prison time, the fact that a movie is scripted for the box office is foretelling of the impact this potential lifestyle has and the impressions it leaves!

Now apply this challenge to a hidden hurt man and he will probably become a villain of his own demeanor and mindset. I have often said that while we all have "some say" in the choices we make, we ultimately have "no say" when it comes to the consequences and correction that most certainly will follow. Isaac Newton's *Third Law of Motion*, states: "For every action, there is an equal and opposite reaction." (PhysicsClassroom.com. 1996-2016). This holds true for things. Especially regarding our personal actions and choices. When the hidden hurt man takes the luxurious leisure stance, it causes added problems to his interactions with others and the solemnity of his own mind.

The competitiveness to be all of these characters portrayed by Denzel Washington, can and most certainly will, crumble a hidden hurt man's heart and image of himself. Especially, when it appears that he is being pulled in different directions by those who want him to fulfill their selfish needs. The hidden hurt man is not Denzel. There are no cameras to shoot his epic and heroic story. He is who he is, in all of his glory, faults and flaws. The only thing he longs for is to know himself, to discover who he is and to figure out what his next move is in life.

Is the true order of life for a Christian, God, family and church or are there other factors occupying his life at this moment? Does he need to change jobs, friends and associates? If so, which should he begin with first? Is he in need of taking one day at a time to develop who he really is or can he plan his life out in increments through progressive self-therapy?

Asking these important questions can help a hidden hurt man do well in life if he takes the appropriate time to know and answer each one. Although the Bible cautions us to: *"Take therefore no thought for the morrow: for the morrow shall take thought for the things of itself..."* (Matthew 6:34), there still is this plaguing resolve to try and project an outcome suited for one's on pleasures. As we near the end of this book, it is my prayer that every hidden hurt man will be rescued and delivered from further hurt that result in more hiding.

CHAPTER: 8
DAMN THE MAN CAVE

According to Wikipedia, a "man cave" or "man space" is a male sanctuary in a home, such as a specially equipped garage, spare bedroom, media room, den, or basement. It is a metaphor describing a room inside the house where "guys can do as they please" like a caveman, without fear of upsetting any female sensibility about house decor or design." (Merriam-Webster, Inc., 2015-j). That sounds real nice to someone who is not taking a true assessment and analogy of what this private space is really doing for men in general and even worse to the hidden hurt man. So, let us spend time unveiling some of the critical aspects of this popular concept, starting with the following question: How is it that the house which was once defined as a man's castle get reduced to him finding solace in only one room that is now depicted as a cave?

The fact that the man went from a *castle* ("a large fortified building or set of buildings; a massive or imposing house; a retreat safe against intrusion or invasion") to a *cave* ("a natural chamber or series of chambers in the earth or in the side of a hill or cliff; an underground chamber for storage") is telling. (Merriam-Webster, Inc., 2015-k). And if you consider the word "cave" in the context of a verb, the meaning gets even worse: "To fall in or down especially from being undermined; cease to resist; cause to fall or collapse". (Merriam-Webster, Inc., 2015-l).

There are at least seven critical and identifiable problems in suggesting that a "man cave" is a good thing, for a man inflicted with tragedy and hopelessness. The type of hopelessness that follows the hidden hurt man like a plume of smoke similar to the comic strip character *Pig-Pen* created by Charles Schultz. (Wikipedia.com, 2016). A closer look at these seven problems or issues may have us turning our man cave back into its original purpose as a garage, spare bedroom, media room, den or basement.

Problem #1: The Cave Man

In a June 2007 article entitled, *"Cavemen: A Cultural Overview of Stone Age Societies,"* author A. O. Kime wrote: "The fact that Stone Age cavemen didn't record their history is commonly thought to be a matter of intellectual ineptitude." (Kime, 2007). Whether this is true or not stands to reason. Nevertheless, it is perplexing not knowing what happened during the former Stone Age. With the exception of cave drawings depicting that the caveman hunted, conducted burials and drew pictures, we know very little about the people evolutionist claim were the forefathers of our current society.

In an article (April 1, 2012) entitled, *Who Were Cavemen?,* authors Dr. David Menton and John Upchurch proposed the following:

> "As far as stereotypes go, cavemen make easy targets—especially when transplanted into the twenty-first century. Their brutish way of dealing with contemporary situations earns a laugh on commercials and TV shows. They just don't understand us modern humans, and their

misunderstanding strikes humor gold. But when we cut away the laugh track and the bumbling ways, we're left with something of an enigmatic figure—a being without a settled place in our understanding of history. Perhaps, in fact, it's our discomfort with not knowing what to do with cavemen that makes us laugh. So, just who were they?" They go on to say, "Before we go spelunking, we need to limit our scope somewhat. At its most basic, the term caveman simply means "a person who dwells in a cave," which isn't unheard of even today. But that's rarely what we mean when we use the word. Instead, we're usually talking about a group of ancient cave hoppers who left behind animal artwork, rough-hewn weapons, and bones—at least, that's the common assumption. While the collective opinion of history and science has moved beyond considering these early humans as animal-like brutes, the term still carries with it the baggage of a being somewhat lesser than modern Homo sapiens." (Menton & Upchurch, 2012).

In my humble opinion (and you may see things differently), having a man cave in the house that is supposed to be your castle, entreats the thought process that a man is returning to some dark period of time when life was not as organized and social interaction was bleak. Why in the world would a hidden hurt man who is already challenged by his lack of emotional security, want to go back to a self-constructed cave for the sole purpose of having a place that defines him as a social outcast? What good could ever come out of this daily visitation that encourages questions like: I don't know what he does in there and I don't really care.

Whatever "king-like" image the man did have in his own castle has been reduced to a man cave dwelling. Besides, whoever heard of a King living in a cave? Even the Prophet Samuel's record of David hiding in the Cave of Addullam (I Samuel 22:1:2) was temporary, to gather his thoughts and regroup his followers. It was never meant to be a place of domain within his castle! By the way, even the name *Addullam* (meaning *refuge*) implies a temporary resolve and not a permanent solution.

Problem #2: Family Separation

The one topic that has been implied throughout this book but now requires its own platform is the family's response to a hidden hurt man living among them. If the hidden hurt man bears the title of husband, father or provider of the household, then this heightens his struggle all the more. One of the first visible signs and effects of a man cave is that it will (without excuse) separate the members of the family. Allow me to explain what I mean. By the 21st century, nearly every home in America had subscribed to some form of social separation. Gone are the days when the family gathered at the dinner table, between 5:30 and 7:00 pm, and all ate the same meal. Gone are the days when the "big TV" was in the den and the family watched it together until the children went to bed. Gone are the days when no one was left behind on a family outing simply because they wanted their own private personal space. But that is not the case today. Today, the entire family structure centers around independence and isolation. The idea of a man barricading himself behind closed doors in a man cave, at the exclusion of his family, does nothing to bring a family together.

We have grown so accustomed to analyzing every issue in the home and prescribing a medication to address it that we rarely see family members together anymore. What we have now is a "stop by the kitchen, get a bite to eat, proceed to your room, watch some cable television and engage in some social action, reaction, or interaction on the iPhone" type of mentality. But I say, put the iPhone down, turn off the cable television, come out of your room, sit down at the dinner table and enjoy some family time. Case in point: I personally know of a family who rarely engage in verbal conversation in the home. Instead of walking into the next room to talk to someone, they communicate with each other by cell phone and text messaging. Scientists describe this type of social interaction as "technological advancement" but I call it "catastrophic consequences, contaminated by careless consciousness." This type of consciousness encourages the "touching of buttons" with our fingers rather than the "touching of each other" with our hands.

The home that was once defined as a man's castle has been transformed into a house filled with dungeons and separated caves for every member of the family. Sadly, we are more accustomed to bonding with our pets than bonding with each other as husband and wife, parents to child and sibling to sibling. Therefore, the phrase, "damn the man cave" is very appropriate for the times we are living in.

Problem #3: The Sinfulness of the Cave

"The [basis of] judgment [an indictment or test by which men are judged] lies in this: the Light has come into the world, and people have loved the darkness rather than and more than the Light, for their works (deeds) were evil. For every wrongdoer hates (loathes, detests) the Light, and will not come out into the Light but shrinks from it, lest his works (deeds, activities, conduct) be exposed and reproved." (John 3:19-20, AMP).

Although I typically write from a Biblical-Psycho-Social approach, it is important to shed light on the outcome of the man cave as a place where men are so shrouded in secrecy and privacy that it leads to sin. Case in point: In the days of my youth, my cousins and I would play behind closed doors, engaging in all sorts of ill-advised activities and mischief. Some of our activities included pushing and shoving matches, looking through Playboy magazines that had been hidden by one of our older cousins and having conversations about things we would never say in front of an adult. Every so often, my grandmother would check in on us by yelling, "What are you boys doing in there?" I never understood why she would constantly do this back then. As an adult man, I now understand the logic of her persistence. It was her way of keeping us in check and out of trouble. Instinctively, she understood the reality that things done in secrecy and privacy often lead to mischief and sinful acts and actions.

Likewise, a hidden hurt man who is already emotionally imprisoned can be easily lured into an even greater place of unimaginable atrocity within the confines of the man cave. The greater a man's privacy and secrecy, the more likely he is to engage in some ill-fated behavior and dark-related sin just waiting to rear its ugly head. Regardless of whether his lure is a sexual draw to an internet porn site or a seemingly innocent visit to a chat room, wherever there is a prolonged state of personal private darkness there will be an inclination towards sin. Do not be deceived into thinking that there is no real person lurking behind these sites, with real motives and inclinations to make a profit off your emotional cravings. There are phone numbers to call with a friendly listening ear, where you can unload your emotional frustrations. There are those so-called friends who beckon you to make a late night stop before you make your way home. You know, the ones who carry your secrets since you stopped sharing the bed with the queen of your castle. Yes, the quiet of the man cave can prove fatal in a man's efforts to bridge the bond of family ties, literally draw him further away from the closeness he once had with his family. All because a degree of sinfulness has penetrated a man's soul and spirit while in the privacy of his personal cave.

Problem #4: The Battle of Domestic Power

It is believed that a woman (the wife) has substantial authority when it comes to designing and decorating the home. But when it comes to decorating a man's personal space and what gets "mounted on the walls" she generally has no say. Since it is accepted that a woman has the greater input when it comes to decorating a house, the man cave in a sense may be a reactionary response to feminine domestic power. How does a woman achieve "domestic power" in a place that a man regards as his castle? Herein lays the confusion between who really has the power in the castles versus the cave.

This is not to suggest that I am promoting a chauvinistic view. After all, I have been married to my lovely wife, Kay, since January 1, 1994; and completely understand a woman's and wife's role in the home, particularly after putting in nine or more hours at work. What I am saying is that the struggle for power in the castle could explain his desire for his own personal space and a retreat into the man cave. And who determined that the terminology of "domestic" should be solely a feminine responsibility? How do you define it in the case of a single man living at home and how does the word domestic relate to him? Truthfully speaking, the word "domestic" does not, nor should it ever be regarded as a feminine term.

In my personal opinion, power in the home is determined by the person who is the primary "voice of the house." This is probably where the entire problem had its creative roots. Think about it. How many times has the father made a decision (or spoken for the house), only to have his decision undermined by the voice of his wife? When I was growing up, I would often hear mothers say things like, "Child, don't worry about what your father just said. I'll talk to him and fix this situation." Trying to prove yourself worthy and accountable as a man, while fighting against societal pressures designed to kill your character, is the last thing a hidden hurting man needs. Sometimes the argument for castle prominence starts with a simple misuse of where he likes to leave his shoes, as opposed to another man's well organized closet. This may seem like a trivial matter under the guise of redecorating but to a hidden hurt man in crisis, feeling lost in his own castle can lead to a longing for comfort and consolation in the warmth of a man cave. In the man cave he can at least be assured that the only voice being spoken and adhered to is his.

Problem #5: The Place of Insecurity

Insecurity is probably one of the greatest hindrances known to man. Especially, when you understand that your God-given purpose is to provide strength and substance. Any man who buys into the concept that they are created in God's image and likeness (Genesis 1:26) will not give space to doubt and insecurity. According to Wikipedia, insecurity implies a lack of confidence in one's ability to do things well.

How many times have you watched episodes of *Criminal Minds* and noticed the insecure behavior of some of the characters. Almost without fail, these individuals retreat to some isolated place or small corner of the room where they feel safe and protected against the world. I use this example, not to point out their idiosyncrasies, but rather to present us with a mental picture of how the man cave functions as a safety zone for the hidden hurt man.

By nature, a room cannot change its properties, purpose or design. Only the person who occupies the space can creatively change and design what it will ultimately be. The man cave, for the insecure hidden hurt man, represents a place of "security and serenity." So long as the hidden hurt man allows insecurity to feaster within him, the man cave will only serve to encourage more hiding and separation from his family and the world.

Problem #6: The Haven of Isolation

When the man cave becomes something more than a hiding place and is converted into a haven (a sheltered place used for rest, shelter or protection) it speaks to a far larger problem for the hidden hurt man because it implies a form of evolutionary adaptation. Evolutionary adaptation happens over a period of time and ultimately leads to complete isolation from others. Whenever the man cave graduates to the status of a haven of isolation, something has gone terribly wrong and is in danger of getting worse.

This brings us back to our original question: "How does a house that was once considered to be a man's castle gets reduced to single room and place of solace called a man cave? Well, if we go back to the earliest accounts of biblical history, we discover God's observation of Adam's existence:

> "Now the Lord God said, It is not good (sufficient, satisfactory) that the man should be alone; I will make him a helper meet (suitable, adapted, complementary) for him." (Genesis 2:18, AMP).

If God concluded that a man needed to be in relationship with someone other than himself, then imagine the significance of a man not being isolated from others in a man cave. The more important question a hidden hurt man needs to ask is how he got into this traumatic place of isolation in the first place. In the great scheme of God's intentional design for man, isolation was frowned upon. Creative words like love, friendship, companionship, relationship, compassion, humor, laughter, fun, and enjoyment were never meant to be solo terms. To the contrary, these are words that were meant to be shared and promoted through a man's partnership with other people and not to be experienced alone or in isolation.

If you find yourself in a place of isolation right now—away from family and the world—then stop what you are doing, get out of that man cave, and say hello to someone in your house! If no one is home, then pick up the phone, reach out to someone and embrace the gift of partnership in your life! Damn the man cave, for it is trying to isolate you from your family!!

Problem #7: The Man Cave Imprisonment

Imprisonment implies confinement. As an ardent movie watcher, I have seen a lot of prison movies like, *The Shawshank Redemption, Cool Hand Luke*, and my all time favorite, *"Life."* The one common element in any good prison movie is the reality of a place called "the hole." This place of solitary confinement is the most inhumane and difficult aspect of the prison experience.

In an article entitled, *Prison Culture*, dated July 18, 2011, a prisoner named Ahmad Al Aswadu is said to have written an essay for the Black Scholar (April-May 1971 issue) called, *A Black View of Prison*. (Aswadu, 2011). The essay describes in great detail the experience of living in the "hole" while incarcerated. This is what he wrote:

> The "Hole" (called such because its locality is usually under the prison's first floor) is solitary confinement. One could stay in the hole for a week or a lifetime depending upon his color and attitude. It is here in the hole that men are made and broken at the same time. It is here that the previous threat of getting "hurt" can realize itself all too quickly. And it is here that the seeds of Black Consciousness have been cultivated in the minds of many black men.
>
> It is very difficult for a layman such as me to describe the atmosphere of the hole but I shall try. I believe that the very first thing that the brother notices about the hole is the desolateness and the feeling of utter aloneness. The first time that I was sent to the hole I felt as if my soul had deserted me. I don't believe that I had ever experienced such a feeling of intense emptiness in my life before then. I had been sent to the hole to have my attitude changed, because, as they stated, it was not conducive to "good order." A brother had just been murdered by the guards who worked in the hole, and rather than go through that type of thing, I pretended to be institutionalized. Fortunately, my stay only lasted fourteen days and I was returned to the general inmate population.

Life in the hole is epitomized by one big question mark. Uncertainty is the order of the day. Your visitors are turned around at the gate when they come to see you. The food quantity and quality is drastically reduced to the level of subsistence. You might get a shower and you might not — depending upon whether or not the guard's wife was good to him the night before. I believe that it is the hole that is the most memorable aspect of the prison experience. They are all the same, and yet they are totally different from one another.

So, what happens when the man cave of a hidden hurt man becomes his "hole" of imprisonment? Will the "hole" institutionalize his effectiveness to be productive? Will it reduce his ability to overcome the skeletons haunting him from the closet of his emotions and mind? Will the rest of his household—his wife, children and friends—stand idly by and allow the man cave to break him? These are questions that need to be answered by those men who live in a castle but long for the frequency of the man cave. May the man cave be forever changed into a recreational room, where the entire family can find solace from the rat race of everyday life. Plaster the walls with pictures of the family, so the temptation of personal privacy does not lure you into a desert of uninhabited and uncultivated thoughts of mischief.

Dear hidden hurting man: The castle is yours. No one is trying to take it from you but you will need to restate your claim as a man. Even if you are still struggling with emotional challenges, you can no longer afford to allow the man cave to isolate and imprison you from the members of your household. You need to be seen as a shining example of inspiration—an inspiration that is motivated by the attentive interests of your family. Rest assured this can only happen if you make up in your mind that you will pledge to "Damn the Man Cave"!!!

CHAPTER: 9
THE RELATIONSHIP DILEMMA: THE CRACKED RIB

Six of the most unique and amazing verses found in the Bible are recorded in Genesis 2:18-23. Consider what is written from the perspective of the Amplified Bible Translation:

> "Now the Lord God said, It is not good (sufficient, satisfactory) that the man should be alone; I will make him a helper meet (suitable, adapted, complimentary) for him. And out of the ground the Lord God formed every [wild] beast and living creature of the field and every bird of the air and brought them to Adam to see what he would call them; and whatever Adam called every living creature, that was its name. And Adam gave names to all the livestock and to the birds of the air and to every [wild] beast of the field; but for Adam there was not found a helper meet (suitable, adapted, complimentary) for him. And the Lord God caused a deep sleep to fall upon Adam; and while he slept, He took one of his ribs or a part of his side and closed up the [place with] flesh. And the rib or part of his side which the Lord God had taken from the man, He built up and made into a woman and He brought her to the man. Then Adam said,

> this [creature] is now bone of my bones and flesh of my flesh; she shall be called Woman, because she was taken out of a man."

Being lonely and alone is a hidden hurt man's worst nightmare. What is so intriguing and extraordinary about the above passage is it not only reveals an apparent problem and flaw in the man but also a Godly solution and remedy to the problem. The problem, as God saw it, was that Adam was both "lonely" and "alone." He was "lonely" in the sense of experiencing sad feelings from being apart from others like himself; and he was "alone" in the sense of being without anyone or anything like himself. In response, God made provision for Adam's needs by creating another like him—a female "help meet" and opposite of him.

If we derive nothing else from the above passage, it is that man does not function well without a support system in place. James E. Talmage, in his article entitled, *Women in Scriptures* (November 9, 2010), stated the following:

> In Hebrew the two words that "help meet" are derived from are the words "ezer" and the word 'k'enegdo". *Ezer*, which is commonly translated as "help" is really a rich word with a much deeper meaning. In her book, Eve and the Choice Made in Eden, Beverly Campbell explains, "According to biblical scholar David Freedman, the Hebrew word translated thee into English as "help" is *ezer*. This

word is a combination of two roots, one meaning "to rescue", "to save," and the other meaning "to be strong." Just as the roots merged into one word, so did their meanings. At first *ezer* meant either "to save" or "to be strong," but in time, said Freedman, "ezer" was always interpreted as 'to help' a mixture of both nuances."

Diana Webb, in her book, Forgotten Women of God, also clarifies this word by explaining, "The noun ezer occurs 21 times in the Hebrew Bible. In eight of these instances the word means "savior". These examples are easy to identify because they are associated with other expressions of deliverance or saving. Elsewhere in the Bible, the root ezer means "strength... the word is most frequently used to describe how God is an ezer to man."

For example, the word "ebenezer" in 1 Samuel 7:12 is used to describe the power of God's deliverance. "Eben" means rock and "ezer" means "help" or "salvation". Ebenezer therefore means "rock of help" or "rock of salvation". The root "ezer" is the same word that God used to describe to Adam who Eve was. She was not intended to be just his helper or his companion, rather she was intended to be his savior, his deliverer.

The other part of the term "help meet" which is commonly translated as "meet for" or "fit for" is the word "k'enegdo". It is hard to know exactly what the word k'enegdo means because it only appears once in the entire Bible. Yet Diana Webb explained that, *"Neged, a related word which means "against", was one of the first words I learned in Hebrew. I thought it was very strange that God would create a companion for Adam that was "against" him! Later, I learned that kenegdo could also mean "in front of" or "opposite."* This still didn't help much. Finally I heard it explained as being "exactly corresponding to," like when you look at yourself in a mirror.

Eve was not designed to be exactly like Adam. She was designed to be his mirror opposite, possessing the other half of the qualities, responsibilities, and attributes which he lacked. Just like Adam and Eve's sexual organs were physically mirror opposites (one being internal and the other external) so were their divine stewardship designed to be opposite but fit together perfectly to create life. Eve was Adam's complete spiritual equal, endowed with a saving power that was opposite from his. (Farrell, 2010).

Now, if we hold Talmage's article as truth (and I choose to do so, or at best, agree that it makes perfectly good sense), then the question becomes, "What happens when a hidden hurt man's rib becomes cracked?" When the one support God created to help assist a hidden hurt man has become "cracked," then where does she go and who does she turn to? This particular concern is by far the greatest of all the chapters and theories previously introduced. It is greater than the theories behind "I'm Sick of Denzel", "Damn the Man Cave", "Sex: The Painful Outlet" and even "Boys Night Out." Herein the ultimate twist: What do you do when what you originally thought to be the truth actually turns out to be something entirely different? In other words, when I speak of Adam's "cracked rib," I am not referring to his "help meet" being insufficient in her abilities to be what he needs. I am referring to the moments when the hidden hurt man's struggle has become so great that his "help meet" becomes emotionally damaged and injured as a result of trying to help him deal with his struggles. Who helps the "help meet" when the "help meet" needs help? Sadly, it usually is not the hidden hurt man—the man who is struggling to survive and to remain functional amid a cloud of dysfunctional emotions and unstable alternatives. The question becomes then, how do we help the "help meet" who has become cracked as a result of the pressures attacking her hidden hurt man? The first order of business would be to identify what are the signs of an emotionally "cracked rib," so we know how to recognize the symptoms and remove any doubt as to why the woman feels the way she does:

Difficulty In Breathing – Physically speaking, one of the most common symptoms of having a cracked, bruised, or fractured rib is the difficulty in breathing. Speaking of breathing, how much breath is required in a relationship? A common cliché used by a woman (when she believes she has found the man she is to become a "help meet" to) is, he took my breath away. Remember the 1995 comedy-drama, *Waiting to Exhale?* Here is the introductory plot:

> Navigating through careers, family and romance, four friends bond over the shortcomings in their love lives -- namely, the scarcity of good men. Both as the "other woman," Savannah (Whitney Houston) and Robin (Lela Rochon) carry on relationships with married men, each believing their lovers will leave their wives for them. On the flip side, Bernadine (Angela Bassett) ends up alone when her husband divorces her for his mistress. Meanwhile, Gloria (Loretta Devine) finds love with a new neighbor. (Waiting to Exhale, 1995).

In essence, they were all in some way or another searching for the type of relationships that felt as natural as breathing. But when a woman's rib is emotionally "cracked" she will find it hard to breathe as a result of some of the struggles her hidden hurt man is experiencing. Grasping for breath is no laughing matter. It disrupts the even flow of her will and excitement to function. It has a trickling effect into other areas of her life and activities. As James Talmage previously stated, when a hidden hurt man's complete spiritual equal experiences a cracked rib and that cracked rib effects her breathing (i.e., the source of her emotional strength, vibrancy, and pizzazz) she will, herself, require a source to derive renewed vigor from.

Exhaustion – Another sign of having an emotionally cracked rib is the "exhaustion" that comes along with having trouble breathing. The tasks and assignments assigned to the woman who is a "help meet" can become quite burdensome as she tries to fulfill the obligations of her wedding vows. Even in perfect marriages, women (wives) become "exhausted" as a result of the common struggles shared with her husband—struggles based in the penalty ascribed to Adam's sin in the Garden of Eden:

> "And unto Adam he said, Because thou hast hearkened unto the voice of thy wife, and hast eaten of the tree, of which I commanded thee, saying, Thou shalt not eat of it: cursed is the ground for thy sake; in sorrow shalt thou eat of it all the days of thy life; Thorns also and thistles shall it bring forth to thee; and thou shalt eat the herb of the field; In the sweat of thy face shalt thou eat bread, till thou return unto the ground; for out of it wast thou taken: for dust thou art, and unto dust shalt thou return." (Gen. 3:17-19, KJV)

Can you imagine the increased stress place upon a woman dealing with the struggles of a hidden hurt man, who not only bears the curse of Adam's struggles but also the crippling struggles of his own? How can a relationship survive this level of attack on marital relationship or friendship that was meant to be a compliment to each other? How can a woman (wife) recover from an attack that challenges her commitment to be there for him? I contend there are at least three commitments a man needs to provide to the woman (his rib):

R (Relationship Responsibility)

We are living in a time when society has done its best to throw responsibility out of the window when it comes to relationships. The one thing we all must hold fast to is commitment, especially with regards to the bonds of marriage. Even in the midst of other relationships, friendships and partnership acquaintances, there must be a resurgence of commitment to one another. Today's wedding vows may have been altered somewhat but there remains a constant when it comes to the promises shared between a man and woman: "For better or for worse; for richer or for poorer; in sickness and in health; until death do us part." This is the responsibility associated with remaining faithful to the relationship—a relationship that is based on all the reasons a man and woman agreed to become as "one" in the first place.

> "Therefore shall a man leave his father and his mother, and shall cleave unto his wife: and they shall be one flesh." (Genesis 2:24).

The word "cleave" means to adhere firmly and closely to, loyally and unwaveringly. While some Bible scholars suggest that this verse is in response to the man only and not the woman. And yet, it should be accepted and understood as a mutual desire for both the woman and man, if they are to maintain a healthy and strong level of commitment to the relationship.

I (Insatiable Interest)

Insatiable means always wanting more but not able to be satisfied. This word is rarely used anymore but this is exactly what is needed for a woman scarred with an emotionally "cracked rib." Somehow and in some way, she is going to have to be developed in spite of exhaustion and shortness of breath; and even in spite of a "I will never stop being there for him" attitude. These things give her power when she is feeling faint and in seasons of feeling no "might" it increases her strength. And yes, she will need a fervor that buys into his every dream, desire, and wish for a successful life.

For that independent spirited woman that is reading this and thinking, "I'm not chasing after any man," this is not what I am suggesting. I am simply saying that a woman must hold onto the adage that "some things are worth fighting for." Never allow your insatiable interest for a man's success to be snuffed out by his emotional baggage that lessens his effectiveness to be a complete spiritual equal for you. An attack on his manhood is the ultimate make or break adjustment for him and you being there unconditionally could be the determining factor of whether he becomes the man that he was created to be.

B (Barricade Busting)

I attribute a lot of the hidden hurt man's atrocities to Satan's bodacious response to God's question of what is he doing? Job 1:6-12 records the following:

"Now there was a day when the sons of God came to present themselves before the Lord, and Satan came also among them. And the Lord said unto Satan, Whence comest thou? Then Satan answered the Lord, and said, From going to and fro in the earth, and from walking up and down in it. And the Lord said unto Satan, Hast thou considered my servant Job, that there is none like him in the earth, a perfect and an upright man, one that feareth God, and escheweth evil? Then Satan answered the Lord, and said, Doth Job fear God for nought? Hast not thou made an hedge about him, and about his house, and about all that he hath on every side? thou hast blessed the work of his hands, and his substance is increased in the land. But put forth thine hand now, and touch all that he hath, and he will curse thee to thy face. And the Lord said unto Satan, Behold, all that he hath is in thy power; only upon himself put not forth thine hand. So Satan went forth from the presence of the Lord."

Satan knows in placing barricades and barriers in the face of a hidden hurt man's path for success (in marriage, fatherhood, and his creative purpose) that he could defeat or, at best, delay man's divine purpose in life. One of the ways a woman can revitalize her efforts to remain the "complete spiritual equal" for her man is to develop a determination to break through and bust up any blockades, barricades, or barriers she sees coming against her man. This of course serves best through a committed life of prayer as the Apostle Paul suggests in Ephesians 6:12: *"For we wrestle not against flesh and blood, but against principalities, against powers, against the rulers of the darkness of this world, against spiritual wickedness in high places."* Prayer is the key that revives not only her will to be the "complete spiritual equal" for him but it is also key in calling forth that spiritual hedge of protection that surrounded Job and protected him during his trials. If you really want to see and experience the power of fervent prayer, try praying with your hidden hurt man, touching and agreeing as the following passage of scriptures suggests:

> "Verily I say unto you, Whatsoever ye shall bind on earth shall be bound in heaven: and whatsoever ye shall loose on earth shall be loosed in heaven. Again I say unto you, That if two of you shall agree on earth as touching any thing that they shall ask, it shall be done for them of my Father which is in heaven. For where two or three are gathered together in my name, there am I in the midst of them". (Matthew 18:18-20)

Prayer has the ability to revive, renew, replenish, refurbish, rejuvenate, regenerate, rebuild, restructure, and refinish any work that has been damaged by the attacks of life. If we could only trust in the God of our salvation and strength, it will restore marriages, relationships, friendships, and partnerships. Yes, mighty woman of God—you who were fearfully and wonderfully made and created to be a man's "help meet"—there is a powerful renewal of energy that can come through prayer. Before you know it, your exhaustion will be refreshed and your breathing will be back to normal. And then once again, you will be the "complete spiritual equal" to your man. Even though he is struggling as a hidden hurt man, he will draw strength from you—a strength that may very well turn his entire outlook and future around.

CHAPTER: 10
NO MORE HURT: LETTING GOD FIND YOU

In Genesis 3:9-10 records the following words: "And the Lord God called unto Adam, and said unto him, "Where art thou?" And he said, I heard thy voice in the garden, and I was afraid, because I was naked; and I hid myself."

What a beautiful and interesting account of God's love and devotion to His creation. Whenever we find ourselves in a compromising position and feel the need to hide (or in the case of the men described in this book choose to remain hidden) God still calls out to us: "Where are you?" This game of "hide-and-go-seek" is not a game He chooses to play. God's ultimate desire and plan for all of us is to have a close and intimate relationship with His creation. Hiding has never been a part of God's divinely orchestrated plan for our lives. Despite the fact that the hidden hurt man regards it as the safest place for his manly redemption. In truth, if he is to hurt no more and be liberated from the need to hide, then he must be willing to cry out in a loud voice, "here I am, Lord" when he senses the presence of God looking for him.

Now, I fully recognize that not everyone who reads this book will be a Christian. It may interest you to know that I tried my best to write from a Biblical-Psycho-Social viewpoint to assure that no man feels as though I am trying to shove God or religion down their throat. As a matter of fact, I intentionally tried to apply my life experiences as a counselor and pastor, while at the same time making drastic attempts to understand the full dynamics of this game we call life, with all of its uncertainties and schemes.

If you're wondering what a "Biblical-Psycho-Social" approach is, then let me explain: A Biblical-Psycho-Social approach to issues, situations, and circumstances, involves taking into account a person's level of understanding to the principles of Christianity, their own behavior mindset, and the manner in which the environment impacts them personally. While it is not my intent to shove religion or God down anyone's throat, I am reminded of these powerful words from *The Confessions of Saint Augustine* entitled, "Our Heart Is Restless Until It Rests In You":

> You are great, Lord, and worthy of our highest praise; your power is great and there is no limit to your wisdom. Man, a tiny part of your creation, wishes to praise you. Though he bears about him his mortality, the evidence of his sin and the evidence that you resist the proud, yet this man, a tiny part of your creation, wishes to praise you. It is you who move man to delight in your praise. For you have made us for yourself, and our heart is restless until it rests in you.
>
> Lord, help me to know and understand which is the soul's first movement, to call upon you for help or to praise you; or if it must first know you before it can call upon you. But if someone does not know you,

how can he call upon you? For, not knowing you, he might call upon someone else instead of you. Or must you first be called upon in order to be known? But Scripture says: Unless they believe in him, how shall they call upon him. And how shall they believe unless someone preaches to them?

Those who seek the Lord will praise him. Seeking the Lord they will find him, and finding him they will praise him. Lord, let me seek you by calling upon you, and let me call upon you believing in you, for you have been preached to us. Lord, my faith calls upon you, the faith you have given me, the faith you have inspired in me by the incarnation of your Son and through the ministry of your preacher.

How shall I call upon my God, my Lord and my God? For when I call upon him, I am really calling him into myself. Where within me can my God come? How can God who made heaven and earth come into me? Lord my God, is there anything in me that can contain you? Can heaven and earth, which you have made and in which you have made me, contain you? Or is it true that whatever exists contains you since without you nothing would exist?

Since I do indeed exist and yet would not exist unless you were in me, why do I ask you to come to me? I am not now in hell, yet you are there. For the psalmist says: If I descend into hell you are there. Therefore, my God, I would not exist at all, unless you were in me; or rather, I would not exist unless I were in you from whom and by whom and in whom all things exist. Yes, Lord, it is so. To what place do I call you to come, since I am in you? Or from what place are you to come to me? Where can I go beyond the bounds of heaven and earth that my God may come to me, for he has said: I fill heaven and earth?

Who will help me to find rest in you? Who will send you into my heart to inebriate it, so that I will forget my evil ways and embrace you, my only good? What are you to me? Have mercy on me that I may speak. What am I to you that you command me to love you, and grow angry and threaten me with terrible punishment if I do not? Is it then a small sorrow not to love you?

In your mercy, Lord my God, tell me what you are to me. Say to my soul, I am your salvation. So speak that I may hear you. The ears of my heart are turned to you, Lord; open them and say to my soul: I am your salvation. I will run after your voice and I will lay hold of you. Do not hide your face from me. Let me see your face even if I die, for if I see it not, I shall die of longing." (Augustine, 1960, pp. 354-430).

Such powerful and lasting words of wisdom uttered by Saint Augustine. But what excites me most is the fact that even when we become too hurt to seek the face of God and our actions pull away from Him, secluded and hiding from His presence, He looks for us— the same way He looked for Adam, His first creation. This is the surety and conviction that a hidden hurt man can rely on to rescue him from his hiding such that he hurts no more. Why? Because the God of his creative personality is looking for him and will not stop until He finds him. In this context, there are three key principles in God's desire to looking for the hidden hurt man:

Principle #1: God Is Calling You

God is calling out to the man. Looking at the aforementioned text (Genesis 3:9-10), we notice that it starts with these words: *"And the Lord God called unto Adam, and said unto him, Where art thou?"* No matter what road the hidden hurt man has traveled or the place of his hidden destination, God is calling out to him— persistently, consistently and directly.

God is calling out *persistently* because He knows that a casual call will not suffice in pulling the hidden hurt man out of his secret hiding place. If God is to find him there must be a call that occurs or exists beyond the usual, expected or normal time for someone to respond. Hidden hurt men are accustomed to "ignoring" calls that attempt to reach or grab their attention. They have in fact become professionals at avoiding the contacts of a call. And thus, the God who is looking for them chooses to remain persistent in His diligence to reach out to them, no matter how long it takes.

God is calling out *consistently* because He is fully aware that the hidden hurt man has been disappointed in the past by persons who say they want to help but are not always faithful in their pursuits. It is the inconsistency of a person's commitment to help that has the hidden hurt man desirous of not being found or sought after for assistance. They have been "dropped" far too often by those who could not handle the weight of the hidden hurt man's painful journey through life. Like the biblical character, Mephibosheth, whose life story begins with this introduction:

> "And Jonathan, Saul's son, had a son that was lame of his feet. He was five years old when the tidings came of Saul and Jonathan out of Jezreel, and his nurse took him up, and fled: and it came to pass, as she made haste to flee, that he fell, and became lame. And his name was Mephibosheth." (2 Samuel 4:4)

Whether this injury was caused by her falling on him or simply dropping him, the one thing that is clear is the nurse was in a hurry and fearing for her life. And so it is with some of us who have not proven faithful to the hidden hurt man because of our own haste in trying to find an overnight solution to a problem that has been going on for years in the hidden hurt man's life. And so God calls out to him consistently to assure him that He will not drop him or leave him. Deuteronomy 31:6 says it best: "Be strong and of a good courage, fear not, nor be afraid of them: for the Lord thy God, he it is that doth go with thee; he will not fail thee, nor forsake thee."

Finally, God is calling out *directly* to the hidden hurt man because He is an all sufficient God. He does not need to send a messenger to speak on His behalf. Rather, He desires a one-on-one dialogue with the creative being that He wants to pull out of hiding. As is in the case of Adam, He calls him by name, calls him out of hiding and into a place of dwelling. God walking in the garden (Eden) suggests that He is always willing to find the hidden hurt man wherever he may be hiding. It is good to know that there is no place that God is not willing to call him out of, whether the man cave, unhealthy sexual relationships, damaging associations or even in the church.

Principle #2: Responding to His Call

God patiently waits on a response to His call. What a wonderful observation concerning the attributes of God that He is willing to wait on you to answer His call. Far too many times in the life and experience of a hidden hurt man, no one waits for his response. Frankly, let us be honest. The moment we call out to others they may be facing a personal crisis of their own that prevents them from responding to our call. How many times have we watched a movie scene where someone who has been kidnapped, gagged at the mouth, and can hear people call out to them for rescue but they are unable to respond? Is not this the case on occasion with the hidden hurt man? And yet, God has proven Himself faithful in His willingness to wait for the hidden hurt man to. Why is this? Because of His never ending patience, love and understanding.

He is a *patient* God because He is perfect in His timing. If you study the creation story (Genesis 1:1-31), you will clearly see that He creates from a patient mindset; making sure that for each day He creates something that it will sustain and support the next day's creative process. Psalms 86:15, 103:8 and 145:8 all say relatively the same thing: "The Lord is merciful and gracious, slow to anger (patient), and plenteous in mercy." He is willing to wait on a response from the hidden hurt man—a response that informs Him that His call has been heard and gladly accepted by someone who is in need of His assistance.

He is also a God of *love*. His love, which is the strong affection for another arising out of kinship or personal ties has been the basis of every act of God towards His creation. We are all familiar with John 3:16: "For God so loved the world, that he gave his only begotten Son, that whosoever believeth in him should not perish, but have everlasting life." It is a love that is also exemplified through His Son, Jesus Christ, who says to each of us, "This is my commandment, that ye love one another, as I have loved you. Greater love hath no man than this, that a man lay down his life for his friends. Ye are my friends, if ye do whatsoever I command you". (John 15:12-14). It is this love that motivates God to wait on a response from the hidden hurt man, assuring him that His love is also able to rectify all of his ills and wrong doings. As 1 Peter 4:8 (AMP) records, "Above all things have intense and unfailing love for one another, for love covers a multitude of sins [forgives and disregards the offenses of others]."

And most importantly, He is a God of *understanding*. One of the great misfortunes of the hidden hurt man (and many other people who are suffering from emotional pain and turmoil) is that it is often difficult to find someone who understands their plight; without being judgmental or pointing a condemning finger of hopelessness towards them. This is a strong attribute of God, and His Son, Christ Jesus. Further, Hebrews 4:12-16 (AMP) informs us:

> "For the Word that God speaks is alive and full of power [making it active, operative, energizing, and effective]; it is sharper than any two-edged sword, penetrating to the dividing line of the breath of life (soul) and [the immortal] spirit, and of joints and marrow [of the deepest parts of our nature], exposing and sifting and analyzing and judging the very thoughts and purposes of the heart. And not a creature exists that is concealed from His sight, but all things are open and exposed, naked and defenseless to the eyes of Him with Whom we have to do. Inasmuch then as we have a great High Priest Who has [already] ascended and passed through the heavens, Jesus the Son of God, let us hold fast our confession [of faith in Him]. For we do not have a High Priest Who is unable to understand and sympathize and have a shared feeling with our weaknesses and

> infirmities and liability to the assaults of temptation, but One Who has been tempted in every respect as we are, yet without sinning. Let us then fearlessly and confidently and boldly draw near to the throne of grace (the throne of God's unmerited favor to us sinners), that we may receive mercy [for our failures] and find grace to help in good time for every need [appropriate help and well-timed help, coming just when we need it]."

Indeed, He is a God of patience, love, and understanding, which are crucially important attributes to a hidden hurt man desiring to respond to the heralding call of God—a God who is patiently awaiting a response.

Principle #3: Open and Honest Dialogue

God wants an open and honest dialogue with the man. After Adam explains, "I heard thy voice in the garden, and I was afraid, because I was naked; and I hid myself...," God immediately initiates a conversation with him that not only allows Adam to express what happened (even though, like many hidden hurt men do, he plays victim by reason of the blame game), but offers a solution to his problematic dilemma. Let's peep in on the rest of this story:

> "And He said, Who told you that you were naked? Have you eaten of the tree of which I commanded you that you should not eat? And the man said, The woman whom You gave to be with me–she gave me [fruit]

from the tree, and I ate. And the Lord God said to the woman, What is this you have done? And the woman said, The serpent beguiled (cheated, outwitted, and deceived) me, and I ate. And the Lord God said to the serpent, Because you have done this, you are cursed above all [domestic] animals and above every [wild] living thing of the field; upon your belly you shall go, and you shall eat dust [and what it contains] all the days of your life. And I will put enmity between you and the woman, and between your offspring and her Offspring; He will bruise and tread your head underfoot, and you will lie in wait and bruise His heel. To the woman He said, I will greatly multiply your grief and your suffering in pregnancy and the pangs of childbearing; with spasms of distress you will bring forth children. Yet your desire and craving will be for your husband, and he will rule over you. And to Adam He said, Because you have listened and given heed to the voice of your wife and have eaten of the tree of which I commanded you, saying, You shall not eat of it, the ground is under a curse because of you; in sorrow and toil shall you eat [of the fruits] of it all the days of your life. Thorns also and thistles shall it bring forth for you, and you shall eat the plants of the field. In the sweat of your face shall you eat bread until you return to the ground, for out of it you were taken; for dust you are and to dust you shall return. The man called his wife's name Eve [life spring], because she was the mother of all the living. For Adam also and for his wife the Lord God made long coats (tunics) of skins and clothed them." (Genesis 3:11-21, AMP)

Yes, He is a God that is willing to have open and honest dialogue with the hidden hurt man. He knows that "recovery" from any maladaptive behavior—no matter the root cause or source—can only happen through honesty. In the 1992 film, *A Few Good Men*, Lt. Daniel Kaffee (Tom Cruise) asks Col. Nathan Jessup (Jack Nicholson), "I want the truth." Col. Jessup's response was, "You can't handle the truth!" But that's not God's "M.O." ("modus operandi" or "mode of operation") for He rewards our honesty. As my pastoral-mentor, Bishop C.E. Glover, (Senior Pastor and Teacher at Mt. Bethel Baptist Ministries in Ft. Lauderdale, Florida) often says, "God is big enough to handle both you and your problems…issues, grievances, hang ups, and hiccups…and so the truth is what He demands of us."

Hopefully, by now you are saying, "Ok, it may not be so bad to have God searching for me." Or perhaps, "I want to be pulled out of my hiding place." However, the tough question associated with these words are, "But how do I open up to Him when in fact I've perfected the art of closing myself off from dealing with my emotional insecurities?"

John McClain, a long time friend and lead musician for many of my concerts (during my days as a national gospel recording artist, promoted under the Tyscot Records label as *Rev. Melvin Dawson and the Genesis Ensemble*), once wrote a song entitled, "Let God Do the Work." This is not some philosophical play on words on. It will require something on the part of the hidden hurt man. After "surrendering to the will of God," the rest is up to Him.

Surrendering All To God

How does one surrender to God? The following acronym describes it perfectly:

S (Stop): Stop running away from past mistakes and failures, for constant running only delays the divinely appointed time you will spend with God (who is waiting to talk with you).

U (Utilize): Utilize every opportunity to expedite and accelerate the process that gets you back to God. Contrary to the lyrics of *Take the Long Way Home*, written by Roger Hodgson and Richard Davies, a hidden hurt man cannot afford to take the long way home, even though his life may very well fit the lyrics:

> *So you think you're a Romeo*
> *playing a part in a picture-show*
> *Take the long way home*
> *Take the long way home*
>
> *'Cause you're the joke of the neighborhood*
> *Why should you care if you're feeling good*
> *Take the long way home*
> *Take the long way home*

The HIDDEN HURT Man

But there are times that you feel you're part of the scenery
All the greenery is comin' down, boy
And then your wife seems to think you're part of the
furniture oh, it's peculiar, she used to be so nice.

When lonely days turn to lonely nights
You take a trip to the city lights
And take the long way home
Take the long way home

You never see what you want to see
Forever playing to the gallery
You take the long way home
Take the long way home

And when you're up on the stage, it's so unbelievable,
Oh unforgettable, how they adore you,
But then your wife seems to think you're losing your sanity,
Oh, calamity, is there no way out?

Does it feel that your life's become a catastrophe?
Oh, it has to be for you to grow, boy.
When you look through the years and see what you could
Have been oh, what you might have been,
If you'd had more time.

The HIDDEN HURT Man

So, when the day comes to settle down,
Who's to blame if you're not around?
You took the long way home
You took the long way home...

R (Re-Evaluate): Re-evaluate your journey. There had to have been a particular incident that began this sojourn of hurt that led to you hiding. The cartoon character, Bugs Bunny, often gets out the hole declaring, "I knew I should have turned left at Albuquerque." And yet, he never goes back down into the hole to return to the place of his error. Although Bugs Bunny teaches us a lesson in being able to handle whatever situation life finds you in. I have always wondered what would have happened if Bugs would have just corrected the mistake by going back to the place of his wrong turn. So many hidden hurt men are afraid to return to that place of error for fear it may cause even greater pain and/or because of the truth that may need to be shared concerning his apparent error.

R (Reassess): Reassess your purpose and potential. One of the great blessings of God is the fact that He wants to show you your true value based on how He sees your worth. In his song, *The Best In Me*, Gospel Recording Artist, Pastor Marvin Sapp says it this way:

"He saw the best in me,
When everyone else around
Could only see the worst in me...
See he's mine, and I am his,
It doesn't matter what I did,
He only sees me, for who I am...."

Legendary Gospel Artist, Vanessa Bell Armstrong, may have said it best in the lyrics of her song, *You Bring Out the Best In Me*:

> "*I thought that I could make it, thought I was doing just fine.*
> *But when my heart was breaking, you were just in time.*
> *I never knew that I could feel this way, oh what a change your love has made.*
>
> *I thought that I could make it, thought I was doing just fine.*
> *But when my heart was breaking, you were just in time.*
> *I never knew that I could feel this way, oh what a change your love has made.*
> *You bring out the best in me always, I thank you!*
>
> *Oh how I long to see you, there's burning inside, ooh, ooh*
> *Every since I met you, you've been first in my life (you've been first in my life)*
> *You said you never go, I need your love, I want the world to know!*
> *You bring out the best in me always;*
> *(The best) I thank you, (you and I) yeah, yeah, yeah*
> *You bring out the best in me always; (The best) yes you do (in me)*
>
> *If it wasn't for your love, tell me where would I be?*

Never knew so much joy so amazing to me!
When all hope was gone, your love lifted me!
Turned my life around with one touch of your hand!
You bring out the best in me! (The best) Youuuuuu!
You bring out, you bring it out, bring out the best in me
You, you, you, you, you, you bring out boy! Heyyyyyy!

(You bring out the best in me) I love you, I love you, you love me (The best)
You bringing out the joy, (You and I) I got so much joy!
You bring out the best in me
You bring it out, nothing but the best, (The best)
You won't settle for nothing less, (in me) oh yeah
(You bring out the best in me) You bring out the best in me
I'm so glad that you do, that you do, (The best)
that you do, you do, you do (You and I)
Oh you bring out the best (in me);
I didn't know which way to go, which way to turn (The best)
You told me, you would be there (in me) always,
(You bring out the best in me)
Every day, every hour (The best) oh, oh, oh, oh, oh (You and I)

You bring out the best (in me), the best, the best..."

E (Expectation): Raise your personal *expectation* of self. One of the first things a hidden hurt man loses is confidence in himself and his abilities. This lack of confidence begins to be the people's anthem for you, which gives them a reasonable excuse to not extend a helping hand to you. Who in their right mind would expel wasted energy on someone who does think much of himself? Perhaps this is why God speaks with confidence and prophetic boldness when He says:

> "For I know the thoughts and plans that I have for you, says the Lord, thoughts and plans for welfare and peace and not for evil, to give you hope in your final outcome. Then you will call upon Me, and you will come and pray to Me, and I will hear and heed you. Then you will seek Me, inquire for, and require Me [as a vital necessity] and find Me when you search for Me with all your heart." [Deuteronomy 4:29-30.]

> "I will be found by you, says the Lord, and I will release you from captivity and gather you from all the nations and all the places to which I have driven you, says the Lord, and I will bring you back to the place from which I caused you to be carried away captive." (Jeremiah 29:11-14 AMP)

N (New): Accept the notion of being under *new* management. It is a certainty that whoever is in control of the hidden hurt man (leading him into a world of emotional mishaps and unscrupulous decision making that has resulted in him not being the "man" he was destined and purposes to be) needs to be fired! Surrendering unto God implies that you have elected to have Him be the controlling entity of your life. Entering under "new management" gives God permission to be the controlling interest in and over your life.

D (Decrease). Be willing to *decrease* God can increase. In the NA and AA Addiction Programs, you often hear the conviction of the 12 Step Principles and Virtues. Observe Step Principles Number 2 & 3:

Step 2 | HOPE – Came to believe that a power greater than ourselves could restore us to sanity.

Step 3 | FAITH – Made a decision to turn our will and our lives over to the care of God as we understood him.

John the Baptist says it even more assertively in the following scriptures:

> "So they came to John and reported to him, Rabbi, the Man Who was with you on the other side of the Jordan [at the Jordan crossing]–and to Whom you yourself have borne testimony–notice, here He is baptizing too, and everybody is flocking to Him! John answered, A man can receive nothing [he can claim nothing, he can take

unto himself nothing] except as it has been granted to him from heaven. [A man must be content to receive the gift which is given him from heaven; there is no other source.] You yourselves are my witnesses [you personally bear me out] that I stated, I am not the Christ (the Anointed One, the Messiah), but I have [only] been sent before Him [in advance of Him, to be His appointed forerunner, His messenger, His announcer]. He who has the bride is the bridegroom; but the groomsman who stands by and listens to him rejoices greatly and heartily on account of the bridegroom's voice. This then is my pleasure and joy, and it is now complete. He must increase, but I must decrease. [He must grow more prominent; I must grow less so.]" (John 3:26-30, AMP)

.

There can never be any genuine surrender unto God without a decrease of one's own thinking process of how to handle life's challenges. A hidden hurt man has to allow God to become the first interest in his life. As we pastors often say, in relation to the order of importance, it is GOD first, FAMILY second, and the CHURCH last.

E (Earnest): Make *earnest* prayer a part of your daily ritual. While we are all familiar with praying. We say grace over our evening dinner. Our children recite poetry at bedtime: "Now I lay me down to sleep, I pray the Lord my soul to keep..." We acknowledge a Higher Power at every AA/NA group meeting or therapy session. And we point our finger towards heaven after every touchdown or home run, even making light of its true importance.

In the Archdiocese of Washington Journal article entitled, *A Simple But Powerful Definition of Prayer,"* Monseigneur Charles Pope said: "I have read many definitions of prayer. I have been especially fond of St. Therese's description. But one of the nicest and briefest descriptions of prayer I have read comes from Dr. Ralph Martin, in his book *The Fulfillment of All Desire*. Dr. Martin says beautifully, in a way that is succinct and yet comprehensive and inclusive of diverse expression: "Prayer is, at root, simply paying attention to God." (Martin, 2006, p. 121).

Such a wonderful imagery to think of prayer as simply paying attention to God. Imagine that. So simple, yet so often overlooked. In traditional circles, I have heard prayer defined as a "conversation with God." True enough and well attested. But the definition sheds less light since many, while able to grasp the talking part of conversation, are less able to grasp or appreciate the listening part of a conversation. And thus, there can be a lot of emphasis on recited prayers, intercessory prayers, etc., all good in and of themselves, and even required. But when and how do we learn to just listen? Theoretically, a person could recite long prayers but in the end pay little attention to God. This is not usually for malicious or prideful motive but due to the fact that our minds are very weak. Therefore, the definition of "conversation" has its pitfalls and limits.

Imagine how different it would be to go to God in prayer saying, "I am going to go aside now and spend some time paying attention to God. I am going to sit still and listen while he speaks. I am going to think on his glory, rejoice in his truth, and ponder as deeply as I can in his presence."

A hidden hurt man is certainly on his way out of his emotional dilemma when he begins to put forth an effort to earnestly pray to the God of all creation. Soon, after times of sincere seeking after God he will begin to see, feel and sense that the imprisonment of his pain is being released. The Bible speaks concerning this type of release, stating:

> "Is anyone among you afflicted (ill-treated, suffering evil)? He should pray. Is anyone glad at heart? He should sing praise [to God]. Is anyone among you sick? He should call in the church elders (the spiritual guides). And they should pray over him, anointing him with oil in the Lord's name. And the prayer [that is] of faith will save him who is sick, and the Lord will restore him; and if he has committed sins, he will be forgiven. Confess to one another therefore your faults (your slips, your false steps, your offenses, your sins) and pray [also] for one another, that you may be healed and restored [to a spiritual tone of mind and heart]. The earnest (heartfelt, continued) prayer of a righteous man makes tremendous power available [dynamic in its working]." (James 5:13-16 AMP)

R (Right vs. Righteous): Develop a sense of understanding when it comes to knowing the difference between being "right" versus becoming "righteous." Being "right" is probably what started the hidden hurt man into a downward spiral of entanglement in the first place. Surrendering to God establishes a new agenda that galvanizes the interest of the hidden hurt man, to help him focus on things pertaining to righteousness. I have often said that everyone is given the right to choose. With every choice there is a consequence to follow. Sometimes, we have no say in what the consequence will be. Many a people have ended up behind prison bars of confinement as a result of certain consequences that accompanied a choice they thought was "right" (such as the "eye for an eye" theory). Surrendering your will to God's will is the equalizer against making bad choices. For the hidden hurt man, this becomes a way of escape from the clutches of his past.

If these surrendering steps are followed, there is a great hope and an even greater possibility that a hidden hurt man will hurt no more. When that happens, the flood gates of restoration and renewal will come rushing in. His home will experience the greatest of blessings. Now seated in his rightful place, he will take his place as "king of the castle." His marriage will experience a new found romance and heartfelt intimacy that goes beyond the physical to the core of the mind, body, and soul. His children will gain a new respect for their father, as he becomes the poster image of a "real man of action" and hero who lives among them.

His friends will admire the change that allows them to no longer walk around on eggshells. No longer will they act as if they do not see the "pink elephant" in the room. As a matter of fact, he will demand that they speak boldly and unabashedly should he revert back to his old "hidden hurt man" nature. More importantly, he will know that there has been a remarkable change in his life. Rufus H. McDaniel's wrote this beautiful hymn that shares the sentiments of hidden hurting men, who are exiled from hiding and back to their rightful place of productivity:

> *What a wonderful change in my life has been wrought*
> *Since Jesus came into my heart;*
> *I have light in my soul for which long I have sought,*
> *Since Jesus came into my heart. Refrain:*
> *Since Jesus came into my heart,*
> *Since Jesus came into my heart;*
> *Floods of joy o'er my soul like the sea billows roll,*
> *Since Jesus came into my heart.*
>
> *I have ceased from my wand'ring and going astray,*
> *Since Jesus came into my heart;*
> *And my sins which were many are all washed away,*
> *Since Jesus came into my heart.*
> *I'm possessed of a hope that is steadfast and sure,*
> *Since Jesus came into my heart;*
> *And no dark clouds of doubt now my pathway obscure,*
> *Since Jesus came into my heart.*

There's a light in the valley of death now for me,
Since Jesus came into my heart;
And the gates of the City beyond I can see,
Since Jesus came into my heart.
I shall go there to dwell in that City I know,
Since Jesus came into my heart;
And I'm happy, so happy as onward I go,
Since Jesus came into my heart.

It is with great hope and anticipation that enough has been said within the pages of this book to prevent the hidden hurt man from hurting. In the early pages of this book I posed the question, "Does a man hide because he's hurting or is he hiding because he is hurting?" Perhaps, the answer to the question is both. What is most important is that no matter the cause, men need not stay in this condition. You can be freed of the emotional imprisonment as a hidden hurting man and you can live a life and testimony that boasts: "I HURT NO MORE." Blessings be upon your life as you walk in your new freedom!

CHAPTER: 11
THE BONUS TRACK

Every now and then, my wife and I will purchase a CD from one of our favorite musical artists who do a kind gesture for us. After we finish listening to the CD (and just before we are about to eject it from the CD player), we discover there is a "bonus track." On this bonus track is a song that the artist created after the project was completed but before it actually duplicated. Because they want to please their fans, they add this final musical masterpiece.

This is exactly how I feel about this final chapter in concluding how a hidden hurt man can recover from his "ills," allows God to find him, and in turn, respond to God's call. In the course of writing of this book there were a few chapters from my original draft that were excluded from this book. Since they are good subjects, I thought I would provide the reader with a sneak peek into some of the things I would love to have discussed at length. The following four subheads provide some additional insights into the hidden hurt man.

I'm Laughing But It Ain't Funny

The objective of this chapter was to draw attention to the masquerading nature of the hidden hurting man in public; and how he goes to great lengths to prevent others from knowing just how broken and devastating his life really is under the weight of his emotional turmoil and pain. The chapter mirrors, if not parallels, the chapter, "Where Do Our Tears Go." My goal was to discuss how the hidden hurt man wears a smile on his face but never shows his true feelings and hurting emotions. Men have grown accustomed to laughing to keep from crying (or exploding). It is often difficult to find an outlet that will give a man the freedom to just let it all hang out. His woman needs a "strong" man. The women on his job or living in his community admire a "confident" man. And the men in their competitiveness will only accept a "humorous" man. So, the hidden hurt man just laughs morning, noon, and night, hoping no one will discover that he is really Clark Kent (or perhaps, Jimmy Olsen) and not Superman.

A Bomb Is Ticking Inside

The goal of this chapter was to shed light on the inner struggle that hidden hurt men often experience in doing their best to not become violently explosive. There is absolutely nothing good that can come out of a man who is filled with anger and deep-rooted depression. Many relationships have suffered at the hands of a man who becomes so angry that he "loses it" at the most inopportune time. The trickle-down effect of his actions can cause so many other mishaps within his life and family. In an article entitled, *Moving Victims of Violence from Crisis to Confidence,* Safe Horizon, (www.safehorizon.org) identifies the following statistics in relation to domestic violence:

- Domestic Violence is a pattern of behavior used to establish power and control over another person through fear and intimidation, often including the threat or use of violence.

- Other terms for domestic violence include intimate partner violence, battering, relationship abuse, spousal abuse, or family violence.

Who Is Most Likely to Suffer from Domestic Abuse or Become a Victim of Domestic Violence?
- Domestic violence and abuse can happen to anyone, regardless of gender, race, ethnicity, sexual orientation, income, or other factors.
- Both women and men can be victims of domestic violence.

How Many Men are Domestic Violence Victims?
- Men are victims of nearly 3 million physical assaults in the USA.

How Often Does Domestic Violence Occur?
- 1 in 4 women will experience domestic violence during her lifetime.

Why Does Domestic Abuse Happen?
- No victim is to blame for any occurrence of domestic abuse or violence.
- While there is no direct cause or explanation why domestic violence happens, it is caused by the abuser or perpetrator.

When and Where Does Domestic Violence Occur?
- Domestic violence is most likely to take place between 6 pm and 6 am.

- More than 60% of domestic violence incidents happen at home.

What Happens to Victims of Domestic Violence?
- Domestic violence is the third leading cause of homelessness among families, according to the U.S. Department of Housing and Urban Development.
- At least 1/3 of the families using New York City's family shelter system are homeless due to domestic violence.

Domestic Violence in America: General Statistics and Facts
- Women ages 18 to 34 are at greatest risk of becoming victims of domestic violence.
- More than 4 million women experience physical assault and rape by their partners. 1 in 3 female homicide victims are murdered by their current or former partner every year.

What are the Effects of Domestic Violence on Children?
- More than 3 million children witness domestic violence in their homes every year.
- Children who live in homes where there is domestic violence also suffer abuse or neglect at high rates (30% to 60%).
- Children exposed to domestic violence at home are more likely to have health problems, including becoming sick more often, having frequent headaches or

stomachaches, and being more tired and lethargic.
- Children are more likely to intervene when they witness severe violence against a parent – which can place a child at great risk for injury or even death.

What are the Effects of Domestic Violence on Mental Health?

- Domestic violence victims face high rates of depression, sleep disturbances, anxiety, flashbacks, and other emotional distress.
- Domestic violence contributes to poor health for many survivors including chronic conditions such as heart disease or gastrointestinal disorders.
- Most women brought to emergency rooms due to domestic violence were socially isolated and had few social and financial resources.

What is the Economic Cost of Domestic Violence?

- Domestic violence costs more than $37 billion a year in law enforcement involvement, legal work, medical and mental health treatment, and lost productivity at companies.

What Happens if Domestic Violence Victims Do Not Receive Help?

- Without help, girls who witness domestic violence are more vulnerable to abuse as teens and adults.

- Without help, boys who witness domestic violence are far more likely to become abusers of their partners and/or children as adults, thus continuing the cycle of violence in the next generation.

When there is a bomb ticking inside a hidden hurt man, it sometimes explodes onto everyone around him. If you believe that you are a man on the brink of exploding or you consider yourself as a potential "ticking time bomb," then do not hesitate to call for help through the Domestic Violence Hotline at (800) 621-HOPE (4673). The service is free, anonymous and available 24 hours a day, seven days a week.

There's No Doctor for This: The Fear of Seeking Help

One of the great tragedies of life is the choice to suffer even when there is help available. It is even more tragic when a hidden hurt man refuses therapy because he regards it as taboo. His general response is, "Counseling is for crazy people and I'm not crazy." Therefore, the likelihood of him *not* receiving help, even though he needs it, becomes very apparent. It is also not a decision that he is likely to come up with on his own. Society itself is a perfect reason men often fail to seek help. Sometimes it is viewed as a weakness for men to go to therapy.
I understand this first hand as a result of my own experiences. Even before my father, Melvin C. Dawson, Sr., died at the young age of 39 of heart attack (and was hospitalized for a period of time for congestive heart failure) I was taking certain medications on a consistent basis. I did my very best to stay healthy but in my mind I believed, "There is no doctor for this." When in truth, it

was the fear of being seen as weak. Of course, now I encourage all men to do their very best to break this cycle of fear and to seek help for their problems, whether it be physical (health), psychological (head), or emotional (heart). Life is already "short lived" by men. Let us not be the cause behind us ending our lives before our time. According to an article written by Dr. Robert Krulwich entitled, *Krulwich Wonders*, he states the following:

> "Women, on average, seem to take a little longer to die. But here's what I didn't know: Women, it turns out, don't just win in the end. It seems that women consistently outlive men in every age cohort. Fetal boys die more often than fetal girls. Baby boys die more often than baby girls. Little boys die more often than little girls. Teenage boys, 20-something boys, 30-something boys — in every age group, the rate of death for guys is higher than for women. The difference widens when we hit our 50s and 60s. Men gallop ahead, then the dying differential narrows, but death keeps favoring males right to the end." (Krolwich, 2013).

Although there are many reasons for this, all men and especially hidden hurt men need to know that there is a "doctor for this;" but you have got to make an appointment and, by all means, do not cancel the visit.

The Religion of Self-Preservation

You can make a religion out of anything if you understand its meaning. According to Merriam-Webster's Dictionary, a religion may be defined as "an interest, a belief, or an activity that is very important to a person or group." (Merriam-Webster 2015-m). So when I refer to "self-preservation" as a religion, I am referring to the hidden hurt man's desire to protect himself from anyone who threatens him with change. In other words, he may want to change at times but resists it simply because someone told him that he should. The reality for him is he did not become a hidden hurt man overnight and neither will he change overnight. As such, he develops his own perspective and "religion" about change that upholds the standards of his own creative constitutional bylaws. To better understand how religion functions as a self-preserving theory, consider the following:

R (Rationalism). Rationalism is a philosophy of thought that believes that reason and experience, and not emotions or religious beliefs, should be the basis for your actions, opinions, etc. This is often the reason hidden hurt men have a quick answer in response to why they are in the situation they are in; and why they feel justified in not changing until it is convenient and best for them.

E (Entitlement). Entitlement is a theory that suggests a feeling or belief that you deserve to be given something (i.e., special privileges). This is why some hidden hurt men live as if the world (or at least their family) owes them something. Regardless of whether they have been faithful in their conquest to overcome their emotional drudgery or not.

L (Lustful Passion). Lustful Passion puts the hidden hurt man in an insatiable downward spiral to achieve a goal beyond his reach. Similar to the pattern of thinking that suggests, "seek after it for lustful passion's sake," lustful passion merely leads the hidden hurt man into an abyss of disappointment, especially if he is looking to be eternally satisfied.

I (Inconsistency). When viewed as a religion, inconsistency can give you the image of someone who is probably good at two specific things:

1) A "Stop and Start" work and production effort. He never completes a task, especially one that would make him a better person. This type of behavior in a hidden hurt man helps to promote a never ending saga of incompletion.

2) The "Blame Game". This is the logic and reasoning behind the "Start and Stop" rituals. It is always someone else's fault! The hidden hurt man makes statements like:
- If only I hadn't been interrupted
- If only that person hadn't thrown me off
- If only someone would have extended me a helping hand
- If only I had been left alone to process this on my on

My father use to describe these types as the "woulda, coulda, shoulda" or "I would if I could but I ain't cause I can't" folks. I think we can all agree that we know someone like this!

G (Greed). Greed is "a selfish desire to have more of something" like money, for example. The problem with a hidden hurt man being a victim of greed is that it lends itself to an irrational type of behavior that makes it hard for him to function normally. Greed is not always financially motivated but it can yield, produce and create what German Social Psychologist, Erich Fromm described as "the same bottomless pit which exhausts the person in an endless effort to satisfy the need without ever reaching satisfaction." (BrarnyQuote.com, n.d.). In turn, it connects us to the need to feel morally or socially better than someone else.

I (Intellectualism). Believe it or not, one of the most harmful behavioral traits known to those who suffer emotional pain is intellectualism. Not so much because they are prone to a "devotion to the exercise of intellect or to intellectual pursuits" but because they believe they know everything already. This "I know everything" mentality prevents them from getting the help they need. One of my favorite quotes from the 2006 comedy, *School for Scoundrels*, is when Dr. P (Billy Bob Thorton) says, "How many of you have self-help books? Okay, that's your first problem. You can't help yourself because your "self" sucks!" (School for Scoundrels, 2006).

Most people who pride themselves as intellectuals usually have something that is quite obvious to everyone else except them. It is a dangerous religion to be a committed member to intellectualism, especially if you are a hidden hurt man.

O (Opacity). Opacity means the quality of a material that does not allow light to pass through it; the quality of being opaque (or not transparent), the quality of being difficult to understand or explain. To the hidden hurt man opacity is perfectly normal behavior. In particular, it leads to the "Man Cave" dilemma discussed in an earlier chapter.

N (Narcissistic Negligence). Finally, the craziest facet of this religious theory is Narcissistic Negligence. The name alone says "run for cover!" Narcissism is identified with synonyms like egocentricity, egocentrism, egomania, egotism, egoism, navel-gazing, self-absorption, self-centeredness, self-concern, self-interest, self-involvement, selfishness, selfness, self-preoccupation, self-regard. All of these characteristic traits are focused around self-interest and promotion. When combined with the concept of negligence or the failure to take the care that a responsible person usually takes; lack of normal care or attention, then you are actually referring to a person who literally disregards their own personal needs of affirmation.

Axioms like, "to thine own self be true" are examples and reminders to us all that we should not neglect ourselves. (Shakespeare, 1599-1602). And yet, this appears to be the down trending response to the hidden hurt man who does his best to minimize his efforts to become better. That neglect then begins to trickle onto his family life like streams into rivers. Ultimately causing a breach within the seams of the family's strength and structure.

These are the four chapters that were deleted from the original draft outline of this books' preliminary research and planning. Even if they were actually a part of the writings, it would not have changed the outcome, for "Letting God Find You" is still the best answer to this plaguing issue of being a man who is hiding because he is hurt; or hurting because he is hiding. I hope you enjoyed these small tidbits of thoughts. Should they stir up any thoughts because you identify with them, are struggling with them or simply desire to draw strength from them, feel free to revisit and reread this chapter as often as you like that you might find a resolve for rescue, restoration, and renewal.

REFERENCES

Anderson, Kirsten. 2013, Jan. 4. *The Number of US Children Living In Single Parent Homes Has Nearly Doubled In 50 Years: Census Data.* Blog. https://www.lifesitenews.com/news/ the-number-of-children-living-in-single-parent-homes-has-nearly-doubled-in

Aswadu, Ahmad Al. 2011, Jul. 18. *A Black View of Prison.* Article. In the "Black Scholar: Prison Culture", Issue Apr.-May, 1971.

Arterburn, Stephen; Stucker, Fred; Luck, Kenny; Yorkey, Mike. 2005. *Every Day For Every Man: 365 Readings For Those Engaged In The Battle.* Colorado: WaterBrook Publishing.

Augustine, St. *The Confessions of St. Augustine.* Translated by John K. Ryan. New York: Doubleday/Random House, Inc., 1960 ed.

BrarnyQuote.com. (n.d.) Dr. Erich Fromm. Quote. http://www.brarnyquote.com/quotes/quotes/e/erichfromm391095.

Bevan, J.L. (2004). *General Partner And Relational Uncertainty As Consequences Of Another Person's Jealousy Expression.* Western Journal of Communication, 68, p. 195.

Bringle, R.G. & Buunk, B.P. (1991). *Extradyadic Relationships and Sexual Jealousy.* In K.

McKinney and S. Sprecher (Eds.), Sexuality in Close Relationships, p. 135. Hillsdale, NJ: Lawrence Erlbaum Associates

Dawson, Kay. *Marriage and Family Therapy Workshop.* Held at Cathedral of Praise ICFM, Miami, FL. May 5, 2015.

Dawson, Melvin. 2013. *Man in the Hole: Learning to Appreciate a Season of Obscure Isolation,* Connecticut: Hope of Vision Publishing.

Dictionary.com. 2016. *Jealousy.* Collins English Dictionary - Complete & Unabridged 10th Edition. Harper-Collins Publishers. http://www.dictionary.com/browse/jealousy.

Farrell, Heather. 2010, Nov. 9. *The Real Meaning of the Term "Help Meet."* Blog Post. Women in the Scriptures. http://www.womeninthescriptures.com/2010/11/real-meaning-of-term-help-meet.html.

Guerrero, L. K., Spitzberg, B. H., & Yoshimura, S. M. (2004). *Sexual and Emotional Jealousy.* In J. Harvey, A. Wenzel, & S. Sprecher (Eds.), "The handbook of sexuality in close relationships" (p. 311). Mahwah, NJ: Lawrence Erlbaum Associates.

John Q. Directed by Nick Cassavetes. 2002. American Crime. New Line Cinema. Film.

Kime, A. O. 2007, June. *Matrix of Mnemos.* Article. In Cavemen: A Cultural Overview of Stone Age Societies.

Krolwich, Dr. Robert. 2013, June 17. *Why Men Die Younger Than Women: The Guys Are Fragile Thesis.* Internet Article. Krulwich Wonders.

Martin, Ralph. 2006, Aug. 1. *The Fulfillment of All Desire.* p. 121. Emmaus Road Publishing.

Menton, Dr. David and Upchurch, Dr. John. 2012, Apr. 1. *Who Were Cavemen?* Online Article. https://answersingenesis.org/human-evolution/cavemen/who-were-cavemen.

Merriam-Webster, Inc. 2015. (a). *Jealousy.* http://www.merriam-webster.com/dictionary/jealousy.

Merriam-Webster, Inc. 2015. (b). *Intuition.* http://www.merriam-webster.com/dictionary/intuition.

Merriam-Webster, Inc. 2015. (c) *Prowess*: http://www.merriam-webster.com/dictionary/prowess.

Merriam-Webster, Inc. 2015. (d) *Impotency.* http://www.merriam-webster.com/dictionary/impotency.

Merriam-Webster, Inc. 2015. (e) *Blindness*. http://www.merriam-webster.com/dictionary/blindmess.

Merriam-Webster, Inc. 2015. (f) *Halt*. http://www.merriam-webster.com/dictionary/halt.

Merriam-Webster. Inc. 2015. (g) *Withered*. http://www.merriam-webster.com/dictionary/withered.

Merriam-Webster, Inc. 2015. (h) *Polarity*. http://www.merriam-webster.com/dictionary/polarity.

Merriam-Webster, Inc. 2015. (i) *Pituitary Gland*: http://www.merriam-webster.com/dictionary/pituitarygland.

Merriam-Webster, Inc. 2015. (j) *Man Cave*. http://www.merriam-webster.com/dictionary/mancave.

Merriam-Webster, Inc. 2015. (k) *Castle*. http://www.merriam-webster.com/dictionary/castle.

Merriam-Webster, Inc. 2015. (l) *Cave*. http://www.merriam-webster.com/dictionary/cave.

Merriam-Webster, Inc. 2015. (m). *Religion*. http://www.merriam-webster.com/dictionary/religion.

Meth, Richard and Pasick, Robert. 1990. *Men in Therapy: The Challenge of Change.* The Guilford Press.

Odle, Teresa. 2013, Sept. 16. *Emotional Development.* Internet Article. Learning Resources. http://www.education.com/reference/article/emotional-development.

PhysicsClassroom.com. 1996-2016. *Newton's Laws: Lesson 4 - Newton's Third Law of Motion.* Online Article. In http://www.physicsclassroom.com/class/newtlaws/Lesson-4/Newton-s-Third-Law.

Safe Horizon. (n.d.). *Moving Victims of Violence from Crisis to Confidence.* Internet Article. http://www.safehorizon.org.

School for Scoundrels. Directed by Todd Phillips. 2006. US: Metro-Goldwyn-Mayer/ Dimension Films/Paramount Pictures. American Feature/Comedy Film.

Shakespeare, William. (1599-1602). *Hamlet.* Act 1, Scene 3.

Sharpsteen, D.J., and Kirkpatrick, L.A. (1997). *Romantic Jealousy and Adult Romantic Attachment.* Journal of Personality and Social Psychology, 72, p. 628.

Shimberg, Elaine Fantle. 1999. *Blending Families.* New York: Berkley Publishing Group.

The Book of Eli. Directed by Albert Hughes and Allen Hughes. 2010. US: Warner Brothers Pictures/Summit Entertainment. Neo-Western/Action Film.

TheFreeDictionary.com. 2003-2016. *Impotency.* Farlex, Inc. http://www.thefreedictionary.com /impotency

Training Day. Directed by Antoine Fuqua. 2001. US: Warner Brothers Pictures. Crime Thriller Film.

Thompson, Dennis Jr. 2010, May 14. *What Causes Blindness.* Online Article. http://www.everydayhealth.com /vision-center/what-causes-blindness.

Waiting to Exhale. Directed by Forest Whitaker. 1995. US: 20th Century Fox. American Romance Film.

White, G.L. (1981). *Jealousy And Partner's Perceived Motives For Attraction To A Rival.* Social Psychology Quarterly, 44, p. 24.

Wikipedia.com. 2016. *Pig-Pen.* Retrieved from https://en.wikipedia.org/wiki/pig-pen.